Education
Goes
Outdoors

Frank A. Johns, *Cleveland State* *sity*

Kurt Allen Liske, *Hudson, Ohio* *hools*

Amy L. Evans, *Painesville, Ohio* *hools*

Addison-Wesley Publishing Company

Menlo Park, California · Reading, Massachusetts · Don Mills, Ontario

Wokingham, England · Amsterdam · Sydney · Singapore

Tokyo · Mexico City · Bogotá · Santiago · San Juan

Acknowledgments

Pages 1 and 103: from pages 45 and 95, respectively, in *The Sense of Wonder,* by Rachel Carson. Copyright © 1956 by Rachel L. Carson. Reprinted by permission of Harper & Row, Publishers, Inc.

Silva® and Orienteering® are registered trademarks of SILVA, a division of Johnson Camping, Inc., Binghamton, New York.

This book is published by the Addison-Wesley Innovative Division.

Design: Jill Casty & Company Design Unltd.

ISBN 0-201-20471-1
5 6 7 8 9 10 AL 95949392

Contents

"... thou canst not stir a flower
Without troubling of a star."

Francis Thompson

Preface

This book is a guide for providing learning experiences in the outdoors and for developing an awareness of the environment through exploration with the senses. We feel that the use of the outdoors provides opportunities and resources to motivate students in learning more about themselves and the world in which they live. The book provides teachers with ideas, materials, resources, and techniques to apply the school curriculum to an outdoor setting, whether it be the school grounds, a community resource, or a resident camp.

The first chapter sets the stage for sensory awareness and provides suggestions for teaching in an outdoor setting. Then we present practical approaches for teaching in the outdoors for kindergarten through grade nine. Ideas and plans are presented for teaching language arts, math, art, social studies, and science in an outdoor setting. Every technique presented has been tested with children in the classroom, on the school grounds, or at a resident camp. Both preservice and inservice teachers successfully implemented these methods. The final chapter of the book discusses using the community as a valuable resource in teaching the school curriculum.

Introduction

Outdoor education applies to a wide variety of learning experiences that take place outside the classroom, and to the skills, appreciation, and attitudes needed to obtain maximum satisfaction from outdoor activities. These experiences are a significant part of a complete education and are essential both in vocational and avocational pursuits. It is important for educators to make outdoor education an integral part of the curriculum, not a negotiable frill based on the affluence of a school district. An understanding of how outdoor activities can be incorporated into the regular school curriculum on school grounds helps increase the usefulness of its approach.

The point can be easily made that an outdoor curriculum is vitally important because of the nature of societal change. Urbanization and industrialization have left a great majority of our young people dependent upon a packaged society. Because of a lack of contact with the physical world that supports them, many youngsters are now so removed from the land that they have little knowledge, concern, or appreciation of the outdoors. Many children neither know nor care where the products of their civilization come from or where things go when they are through with them. A loss of contact between the natural world and the many things that can be learned from it has been sacrificed for the safety and convenience of the school building, which in some instances has become a guarded fortress. The predictable school environment has been allowed to become a barrier to many types of learning rather than the organizing force it was intended to be.

The main objective of this book is to convince teachers that the best way to learn about the natural environment is through direct contact with it, whether on the school grounds, at other sites in the community, or at a special outdoor education camp. Students may be intellectually stimulated and even supportive of a point of view through books and other vicarious experiences but still be emotionally unable to accept or come to terms with the natural world around them. As a result, students may have negative reactions—fear of insects, fear of storms, feelings of disgust and disdain—to new sensations in the environment.

Children (and the adults they will become) need the emotional experience of feeling the out-of-doors. This includes using all the senses—taste, smell, touch, sight, and hearing—in a total operation to absorb the various moods of the out-of-doors.

Through this process, attitudes toward and appreciation of one's relationship to the land will be developed. Students' understanding of the physical world that supports them will replace the fear and open hostility that is sometimes evidenced by their behavior.

Many things about the natural environment are learned best when one is in direct contact with that environment. Walt Whitman expresses this beautifully in the following poem:

"There was a child went forth every day;
   And the first object he looked upon,
   That object he became;

And that object became part of him
   For the day, or a certain part of the day,
   Or for many years, or stretching
   Cycles of years."

A second objective of this book is to use the out-of-doors and the natural world to teach the inquiry process. We present a certain reality of the nature of learning: Children will not remain students in a classroom; they will be living in a world that presents innumerable experiences and, consequently, many problems. Each child will be required to respond to these problems in a unique way, using inquiry skills and attitudes to generate, organize, and evaluate knowledge. Our approach helps children find answers to problems that arise in their lives and provides them with an education that is far broader than what the in-class school curriculum can offer.

Inquiry teaching requires that skills and attitudes be developed to give children the opportunity to participate actively in the learning process. As a part of this process, children need to listen to others, participate in group discussions, expose their senses to concrete things in the world around them, read, apply previously learned concepts and principles, develop a vocabulary to describe phenomena, keep accurate records, and interpret their work.

Children should be encouraged to develop a curiosity about the world, to look at things with an open mind, to avoid making decisions until as much evidence as possible has been collected, and to make decisions based on the evidence found.

Activities that use the processes of observing, classifying, describing, measuring, inferring, and predicting build skills that will continue to be important throughout life. Research indicates that students retain more knowledge through using thinking skill processes than through studying factual information or even broad conceptual material. An inquiry approach along with student involvement in a highly affective setting provides an extremely motivating and stimulating curriculum.

A third objective of this book is to develop positive interaction skills among students and between students and teachers. School classes represent an aggregate of individuals brought together at a special time in a specific place. A teacher is assigned to a class and provided with a set of goals and objectives by the board of education, and schooling begins. Within this setting, students learn together and alone using competitive, individualistic, and cooperative skills they have acquired from previous classes and other experiences. Among these skills, none is so important as cooperative interaction.

A broad framework of cooperative interaction is a necessity for competitive and individualistic behavior to occur. No interaction can take place without enough cooperation to establish communication, set norms for behavior, and agree upon goals. The building of this cooperative setting and the development of a cohesive group are important objectives because they provide an excellent environment for learning and a model for future societal relationships.

Group building and cooperative learning take on greater importance in outdoor education because the activities take students to educational settings that are different from the familiarity of the classroom. The exploration of new environments by the students makes positive interaction imperative. With this in mind, ideas for getting the group started, sharing and processing information, teacher dialogue, and student responsibility are presented.

The objectives stated in this introduction are addressed throughout the book, either in the selection of appropriate activities or in the procedures for teaching them. Teachers with their classes have tested all of the ideas in a variety of settings and have found them useful; we hope you will, too. Good luck in your outdoor adventuring!

Sensitivity to the Environment

"I sincerely believe that for the child, and for the parent seeking to guide him, it is not half so important to *know* as to *feel.* If facts are the seeds that later produce knowledge and wisdom, then the emotions and the impressions of the senses are the fertile soil in which the seeds must grow.... Once the emotions have been aroused—a sense of the beautiful, the excitement of the new and unknown, a feeling of sympathy, pity, admiration, or love—then we wish for the knowledge about the object of our emotional response. Once found, it has lasting meaning. It is more important to pave the way for the child to want to know than to put him on a diet of facts he is not ready to assimilate."

Rachel Carson

Rachel Carson beautifully expressed the importance of nurturing in young people a sense of wonder for the natural world and assisting them in observing and feeling more deeply the out-of-doors.

The object of this chapter is to set the tone for outdoor education, from sensitizing individuals to their environment to helping them feel the out-of-doors.

What can teachers do to help children sense the mystery of a forest, feel the crispness of a fall morning, or hear the whisper of an awakening wind? Three areas of activity are presented in this chapter to offer answers to this question and to provide techniques for developing awareness experiences: (1) sensory games; (2) outdoor explorations; and (3) group adventures.

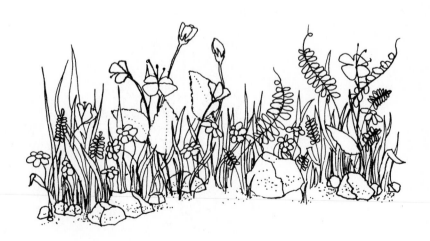

Sensory Games

One need not explain the magic of the word *game* when it is mentioned to a child, a classroom of students, or adults at a party. The word instantly conveys the message of fun and sport with enjoyment as a basic ingredient.

Games are a natural place to begin exploration with the senses. The following excerpt by Virginia Musselman states this viewpoint eloquently:

> We sometimes forget that a child is new. Almost everything he does is a first: the first time he whistles; the first time he lights a fire; the first time he's blindfolded in a game; the first time he learns a new word, feels suspense, or enjoys applause. The first time he sees a butterfly, or snow; or tastes ice cream; or hears a bird sing; or feels the warm softness of a puppy.
>
> Those firsts should be fun. They should lead on to seconds, and thirds, and on and on. They will, as long as that child keeps his sense of wonder.
>
> Childhood, in this age of accelerated maturity, is growing shorter. Pressures are growing stronger. Children need periods of informal, relaxed play more than ever. They need simple, interesting games that provide exercise for growing muscles, stimulation for growing minds, and outlets for growing individualism. Games can do all this and more. Games can provide a contact, a bridge, to bring the child closer to the world of nature.

The games presented in this section begin the sensory exploration process—fine tuning the senses. They will bring to each child a new awareness of the meaning of smelling, touching, seeing, and hearing.

Smelling Games

Night Trails

Divide the group into small teams. Give each team a scent in a liquid form: molasses, mint, pine oil, and so on. After dark, have the teams use the liquid scent to paint separate trails. Tell each group to start from a central point and periodically brush some scent on objects along the way: rocks, trees, stumps, and so on. Have them place a marker at the end of each trail. Once courses are laid out, have the teams return to the starting point, exchange scents, and pursue another team's trail. Follow-up discussions on territorial rights and familial bonds are valuable.

Smell Hike

Can a *smelly hike* be fun? Take the children on a hike around the school yard, neighborhood, or campsite, and see how many different smells they can identify.

Have the children keep a list in the classroom of the smells and where they came from. Add new smells as they are identified. Classification skills can be developed by subdividing the list into categories such as classroom smells, playground smells, forest smells, and street smells.

Sniffer Station

Place substances that have distinctive odors in opaque containers (plastic mustard or ketchup dispensers work well). Number each one for identification.

Have children take turns smelling the contents of each and write down their guesses. Food smells might include some of the following items:

mint	lime	coffee	garlic
peanut butter	tea leaves	onion	cheese
grapes	lemon	vanilla	orange peels
vinegar	cinnamon	chocolate	chili peppers

Other categories for the contents of the Sniffer Station containers could be soaps, spices, plants, and perfumes.

Vary the game by asking students to identify places or things that a smell reminds them of; a pizza parlor, new shoes, or a special toy. Personal experiences can be useful for these asociation.

For another activity, have students find words, such as sweet, musty, and rancid, that describe the smell of given objects. The class could make up a list of all words that can be used to describe how something smells in order to develop vocabulary.

Touching Games

Identification Circle

Select about a dozen items (natural if possible) that are the same. Items such as apples, oranges, leaves, potatoes, or nuts will work well. Have the students form a circle and put on blindfolds. Then hand each of them an object. Items should be numbered so that you can match each student with his or her object.

Ask students to become familiar with their object. Urge them to be aware of slight differences; they will have to identify their own object later on. After two or three minutes, take the objects and place them in the center of the circle. Tell students to remove their blindfolds and see if they can pick out their own object. Make sure children explain to the group how they identified their object to help them use words that describe the sense of touch.

Buster Brown

Pair up students and form a large circle on the ground with space between each pair. Blindfold one member of each pair and have the other remove and present a shoe to his or her partner for examination. Then place the shoes in the center of the circle. When the signal is given, have blindfolded students crawl to the center and work together to locate their partners' shoes. The game is completed when blindfolded students have returned to their places with the correct shoe. There are lots of variations to this game, and with a little brainstorming some new Buster Browns may be created!

Hands

Have six to eight students form a small circle facing outward, their backs to one another, eyes closed, and hands held out at waist level. Have the same number of students form an outer circle, each standing opposite someone in the inner circle. Ask the students whose eyes are closed to become familiar with the hands of the person in front of them.

Once the students in the inner circle feel they know their partner's hand, the students in the second circle move about at random, having their hands "examined" by the students in the first circle. Have students continue to reject hands offered them until they identify the correct pair of hands. Once students correctly identify their partners, they may watch the rest of the activity.

Seeing Games

Trays

Present students with a number of different objects on a tray for 30 seconds, then remove or cover it. Have students list as many of the items on the tray as they can recall. Display the tray again and let them compare their lists with the objects. Have a short discussion of the different strategies they used to recall what they observed. Present another tray and see how well they do. To conclude the experience, show the group a third tray of objects. Once the tray is removed, have students work as a group to compile the list. Conduct a follow-up discussion on the value of shared observations. Another technique is to present a collection of objects to the group; out of their view, remove one of the items, and then have them identify the missing object.

Sharp Eyes

Have the children sit in a circle on the floor. Select one child to be "It." Have "It" leave the group while a captain is chosen. Then have the captain begin to lead the others through a series of rhythmic hand gestures and motions. Have "It" return and take three chances to find out who the captain is. Chanting is sometimes used to spice things up and signal "It" to return to the group. A good chant is Bub-ly-Eye-Kye, Bub-ly-Eye-Kye, and so on.

Eye Catchers

Have students line up in two rows facing one another, each person having a partner about four or five feet across from him or her. Tell one row of students to look over their partner carefully, noting observable characteristics.

After about one minute, tell the observing row to turn around. Then tell the children that were observed to alter two items of their appearance (making a change in their clothing by unfastening a button or changing their hair style in some fashion are examples).

Tell observers to turn around and try to find the two changes. Reverse the procedure to give the other row a chance to try the experience. If there is an uneven number of students, three can work together with each person making one observable change or taking turns and doing the game twice, or you can play along.

If more competition is desired, turn the rows into teams, give points for each correct answer and subtract points for each incorrect guess. The team with the greatest number of points wins.

Geometric Shaping

Give small groups of students (four or five to a team) a series of geometric shapes that when arranged correctly will make five squares of equal size. Have students work together nonverbally to complete the task. (Doing this activity nonverbally ensures maximum group participation.) Provide the students with lots of floor or table space to do this exercise.

Outlined below are the five squares and the geometric shapes used to make each of the squares.

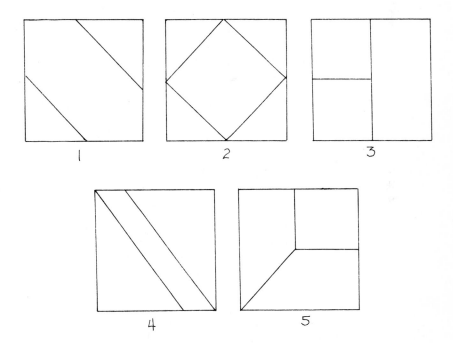

Tag board (laminated if possible) squares of about 12″ are suitable for this activity.

Hearing Games

Call of the Wild

Have students choose partners and select word pairs, such as night/day, high/low, after/before, and so on. Then have each partner take one of the words in the word pair. Separate partners to opposite ends of a field and blindfold them. At the signal, the blindfolded partners seek one another with their own particular "call of the wild." Listening and calling, the partners move toward each other. Once linked up, players can remove their blindfolds and watch the fun.

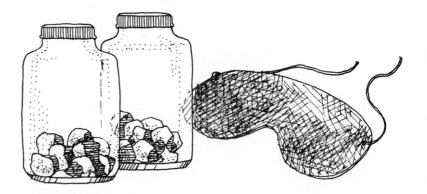

Rattlers

Have students form a large circle to establish the boundaries for the game. Select two players and give them rattlers (plastic pill bottles with stones inside) and blindfolds. Identify one player as the predator and the other as the prey. Blindfold both players and tell them to stay inside the circle. The object is for the predator to tag the prey. Each time the predator shakes the rattle, the prey must immediately respond with a rattle. The predator has a total of five rattles in which to catch the prey. The rest of the group may involve itself more by periodically joining hands and changing the shape of the boundaries, making the circle smaller or larger. Brainstorm with the group on other ways the circle could become involved.

Night Sounds and Prey Beware

Choose one student to be predator and give her or him one distinct sound that is known to the entire group. Divide the rest into pairs and provide them with matching sound makers: two whistles, two drums, two clappers, two sets of sticks, and so on.

After dark, separate all partners across a field or wooded area. At the signal, have partners cautiously use their sounds to seek each other out. A tag of either partner by the predator constitutes a capture. The object of the game is for the partners to find each other without being captured. The predator, upon capturing the prey, must sound his signal; the captured prey thus is silenced; his or her partner is doomed. The partners who successfully link up are in free.

Stalk on the Wild Side

This fun, suspenseful game requires silence and a sensitive ear; it is an excellent follow-up to the game of Rattlers.

Connect three or four trees in a wooded area with rope to form an enclosure. One person is the predator, the other the prey. Blindfold and place each player somewhere along the rope. Walking on the wild side, the stalker must catch its prey. Both players must hold onto the rope, and neither should make a sound.

Have the rest of the group watch in complete silence and plot strategy while waiting a turn. Rope off several playing areas if the group is large.

Outdoor Explorations

The sensory games awakened new feelings in the students—the first step in outdoor education. Through games, their senses have been heightened, putting the students in touch with many new experiences. This first step is important because of the age, grade, and experience differences of the students; it prepares them for a more total commitment to a special school site, land lab, or resident camp.

The emphasis of Outdoor Explorations is to provide more specific discovery experiences in the out-of-doors. For this reason, the phrasing of questions and other teacher dialogue reinforces the sensory experiences provided in this section's exercises by emphasizing description and observation.

Phrasing Questions

Some words used in asking questions, such as *can, does, should,* and *would,* ask for a "yes" or "no" response and usually end discussion. This problem can be eliminated by rephrasing the question, using one of the interrogative forms, such as *how, what, when, where,* or *why.* This questioning strategy is not meant to elicit one word answers or specific technical facts. Therefore, instead of questions such as "What kind of bird is that?" or "Where does it live?" phrase questions that produce a sequence of thoughts. For example: "What do you notice about the way that bird is flying?" or "Why do you suppose that bird has such unusual coloring?"

A number of the described activities have students working as a group or with partners. Therefore, this questioning strategy, with the emphasis on description and observation, should be explained to them. Encourage students to follow the same process when they are working with others. This will reinforce your method, ensuring increased student participation and a more meaningful lesson.

Other Teacher Dialogue

The extension of observations and descriptions into concepts can be accomplished by carefully thought-out questions, as shown in the following examples:

"Notice this large uprooted tree; what do you suppose will happen to all of the younger trees nearby?"

"Look at this section of the ravine; how many examples of erosion can you see and what do you suppose caused it?"

During the exploration of an outdoor site, you can also use some introductory remarks when giving instructions. These may include comparing and contrasting. For example:

"Imagine coming back to this exact spot in 25, 50, or 100 years; tell us how you think this site will look then."

"We looked at the area behind the school this morning; compare it to the place we're at now."

Projecting into the future, as in the first example, can also be used conversely by going back in time. This can be extremely interesting if you have knowledge of the school and the area or if the site has some notable historical background. Interviewing senior residents or doing a little research on your own sometimes produces surprising information about your locality.

Introductory dialogue may include just a few words that help extend the concept beyond observation and description. For example:

"You are visitors from another planet that is completely different from ours. Explain the purpose of the vegetation you see around here."

Younger children especially will enjoy the element of magic or fantasy in your remarks. The "Hundred Inch Hike" activity in this section can be made more enticing and colorful by using questions similar to the following:

"Pretend you are an ant going along the trail. What kinds of things would you have to crawl over?"

"How would that leaf look to you from underneath if you were an ant? Would it be as green?"

Or a statement can be used, such as the following:

"A magic spell has changed you into tiny elves two inches high. As you go along the trail, think of the parts of the journey that would be difficult, dangerous, or frightening to you."

As stated in the beginning of this section, teacher dialogue is an important factor in making the outdoor adventures successful. Stress observation and description while developing concepts whenever you can to ensure a positive and enjoyable learning experience for your students.

Moving into more intense experiences requires increased teacher direction. The activities described in this section require more dialogue in setting the scene and transforming a series of exercises into conceptual learning. These sensory exercises are concise and structured, and unlike the sensory games, you are an important factor in transforming the sensory and ecological experiences into personal awareness. As Rachel Carson stated, "Once the emotions have been aroused . . . then we wish for the knowledge about the object of our emotional response."

Exercises in Outdoor Explorations

Tiny Trails—A Hundred Inch Hike

Give each student a magnifying glass, a spool with 100 inches of string, and ten painted, 4-inch sticks. Select the environment: an edge of a stream, a meadow, a forest floor, a school yard. Have students blaze a trail on their hands and knees. Students crawling on all fours lay out their strings as trails and examine the microworld along them. Students use their sticks to mark unusual objects: tiny flowers, mushrooms, cracks, insect condominiums, colorful shapes. Students should name their trails: "Mushroom Journey," "Bits of This and That," "Shades of Green," "Micro Real Estate," and so on. After the trails are laid out, students reassemble and select partners. Partners follow each trail and share their journeys—fantasies and realities.

Trust Walk

A trust walk focuses on two experiences: heightening awarenesses of natural surroundings and building a trusting relationship between people. Students pair off, and guides lead their blindfolded partners in the outdoors.

The trust building experience might include climbing over or crawling under fences, roots, and branches; walking and running through a field or woods; and crossing a stream or ravine.

Heightening the awareness of the outdoors could involve touching the texture of a tree, feeling a stream's motion, listening to a gentle breeze, or sensing the stillness of a deep woods.

Dialogue between partners is important to the trust walk. Guides should introduce experiences with questions that will encourage their partners to sense more fully their surroundings:

1. How does this tree's bark compare with another?
2. Is the tree still living?
3. Where is the trail's edge?
4. How does the forest floor feel?

Contrast different areas of the walk:

1. Is it colder or warmer here?
2. Is the trail rougher?
3. Is it damper or more moist here?
4. How does this side of the ravine compare to the other?

Such questions enable the blindfolded students to focus on experiences and articulate their thoughts.

Equally important to the trust walk is the mood a teacher establishes. Guides need to sense the significance of their roles, and similarly, blindfolded students need to understand the opportunity they have to explore their surroundings in a new manner.

Each partner should experience both roles, and the time span for the trust walk will vary with grade level—recommended time allotment for upper elementary is 10–15 minutes.

Tree Adventuring

Divide students into pairs; one is a guide and the other is blindfolded. Starting from a central point, have the guides lead blindfolded partners to certain trees in a wooded area. The blindfolded partners carefully explore their trees and articulate to the guides what they are sensing. Observations could include the following:

1. The tree is about five feet around.
2. Bark is slightly ridged.
3. Two small branches are at shoulder height.
4. There are big roots spreading out in all directions from the base of the tree.
5. There is a small opening at the bottom.

As in the trust walk, guides might ask their partners certain questions to increase verbalization of the sensory experience.

After this detailed study of the tree, have the guides lead partners back to a central point and remove their blindfolds. Encourage students again to verbalize their sensory experience. Then have them try to locate their individual trees. Have partners reverse roles and repeat the activity.

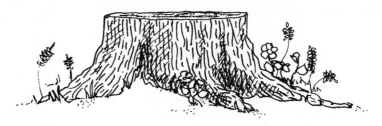

Mystery Circle

A mystery circle is best suited for a setting that is in close proximity to a number of different natural environments—forest, pond, meadow, swamp, stream, and so on. This activity can also be used around your own school where there are a number of different environments. These would include trees, grassy areas, flower beds, driveways, and the softball diamond.

Blindfold a small group of students who are seated in a circle on the ground. Hand out previously collected items from the surroundings, one per student. These items could include the following things:

cattail	staghorn sumac blossom
pine cone	dandelion
piece of slate	acorns
stem from a blackberry bush	thistle
grapevine	rotting wood
feather	stream bed stones

While students are examining their objects, introduce the following questions:

1. What words would you use to describe your object's shape, size, texture, and density?
2. In which of the following environments might this object be found: forest, pond, meadow?
3. What other kinds of objects might you find in the same environment?

Have the group remove their blindfolds and then have students use the above sequence of questions to share and discuss their objects.

In the final phase of this activity, instruct students to explore the immediate surroundings and locate the particular settings in which the different objects are found. All the sudents should have the opportunity to visit different environments and see the objects in their natural settings.

**Life Line
of a Tree**

This activity focuses specifically on trees, their life cycles and environments. In small groups, ask students to examine closely a table full of objects from a tree. These might include:

seedlings of various sizes	nuts
log cross section	pine cones
pieces of bark and wood	leaves
small branches	peat
chunks of decaying wood	forest soil

While the students are examining these materials, encourage them to share their observations and discoveries with each other.

After a few minutes, ask students, "What do all these materials have in common?" Next, challenge the class to work together and place all the objects in a sequence that represents a tree's life line (some groups may end up making a life cycle). Upon completion of this task, ask one or more of the students to explain the rationale for the order of materials in the life line.

Following this phase of the activity and depending upon the kind of life line constructed, ask the group to discuss some of the following questions:

1. Where else might you find seeds and leaves in the tree's life line?

2. (If students made a life cycle) How did the tree's life line turn out to be a life cycle?

3. Do all trees' life lines follow this pattern?

4. What are some ways a tree's life line can be altered?

5. What other materials could be included in the life line?

6. How many years might a tree's life line span?

In the final phase of this activity, have students each select one or two objects from the table and return them to their natural environment. While on this hike in the woods, the group could share their observations on the life lines they see around them.

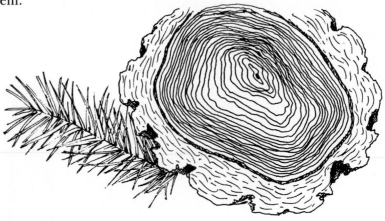

Group Adventures

A typical school classroom is an aggregate of individuals working together or alone using competitive, individualistic, and cooperative skills. Teachers interact with students, using all three skills to meet content area goals. Probably the most basic of these skills is cooperation, because interaction could not take place without enough cooperation to establish communication, set behavior norms, and agree upon goals. Since all competition and individualistic behavior take place within the broader framework of cooperation, a large part of your time is spent making this aggregate a cohesive group.

Group building and cooperative learning are key goals in their own right, but they take on greater importance in outdoor education. The activities described in this book take students to educational settings that are different from the familiarity of the classroom. Many of the environments being explored are new for students, making cooperation an even more important requirement.

Getting the Group Started

The progression of experiences presented in this chapter provides the student with a start toward reaching the goals of the outdoor education curriculum, whether it takes place on the school grounds or at a special resident camp.

As you begin using these activities, the first few processing sessions should be brief. "Processing" is the manner in which information is discussed, clarified, interpreted, and shared. Take only enough time to bring out a few learnings and to allow students to express their feelings about the experience. During these beginning sessions, set the tone of the group by listening more and informing less. Accept comments on things students have noticed without stepping into an authoritative role. Occasional errors of perception or deduction may occur, but hold off from correcting at this point. These errors do relatively little harm and the payoff is greater group discussion and risk-taking in the future.

Sharing Circles and Processing Information

A sharing circle is an excellent way to allow for verbalization of the group's experience and reaction to an exercise. The following steps are suggested while processing information after an activity:

1. Form a circle whenever possible.

2. Ask the students to agree not to interrupt or use put-downs, smart remarks, or other inappropriate comments.

3. Focus questions on the process the students have completed, emphasizing *how, what, when,* and *why* questions, as discussed in the section on "Outdoor Explorations."

4. Allow students time to answer. An increased wait-time on your part will encourage discussion.

5. Allow students to pass on questions while sharing information if they desire.

6. Make comments and ask questions about what was seen or heard without making judgments.

7. Summarize what has been discussed or learned at the end of the processing to help complete the exercise.

The sharing of experiences is the key to successful concept building and to having a productive learning experience. We encourage you to use the sharing circle guidelines, keeping in mind the following hints to continue the group processing. Have the students share their work with the total class by recording field notes on chart paper for display. Hearing oral reports and viewing displays from individuals and groups show the students you value their input, which usually increases participation.

Another technique that works well in promoting discussion is to collect some items during the exercise. You can have students bring back an item such as a leaf, twig, shell, fungus, or some other find related to their activity. To practice good conservation, limit the number of samples picked by designating a particular student to bring back a sample.

The use of door openers also extends the experience of the students and encourages further discussion. Sometimes saying, "Tell me about it," "I'd like to hear your thinking about it" or simply, "No fooling," "You did?" "How about that," or "Really," help initiate, expand, or continue the expressions of thoughts and feelings. At times, use the leading question, "What do you think, Joe?" Mentioning students by name helps to get them involved and conveys the attitude of personal discovery.

The processing of activities could include more than a discussion of ideas and concepts related to the places and things encountered. Examining how decisions were made, including the roles played by the various students, is valuable as a personal growth experience. If you wish to follow this optional type of discussion, it can be initiated with the following questions:

1. "Did you offer suggestions?"
2. "Who was the leader of this activity. Why?"
3. "What are the qualities of good leadership?"
4. "Who had ideas that did not come out?"
5. "Why do you suppose some students were not heard?"

The discussion then begins to focus more on the individuals in the class developing expressions of their feelings and insights.

Promoting discussion and processing the information after an activity is not automatic. A prescriptive set of suggestions is only the beginning as you set the proper discussion-group atmosphere. The format provided by the sharing circle and discussion strategies needs to be practiced, encouraged, and rewarded as you would to elicit any desired behavior. If you stick to it, it will work and will provide rewarding experiences for you and your students.

Exercises in Building the Group

Jam Up

Have a team consisting of two groups of four students each position itself on small squares of cardboard placed in a semicircle (2 or 3 feet between squares). Both groups face each other and are separated by a middle, unoccupied square.

Challenge the whole team to use the following rules to get the group of students on the left placed on the right and the students on the right placed on the left.

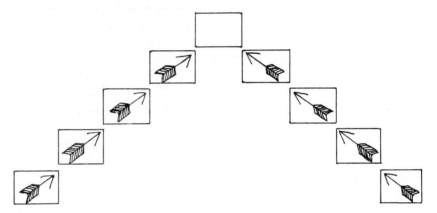

1. A student *may* move onto an empty square in front of him or her.
2. A student *may* move onto an empty square around a person who is facing him or her.
3. A student *may not* move backward.
4. A student *may not* move around someone who is facing the same direction.
5. A move *may not* involve two persons moving at the same time.

Mimics

(This game obviously needs to be handled in a sensitive way. It can provide an excellent follow-up to *Story of My Life,* by Helen Keller.)

Divide the class into two groups. The students in first group role play persons who are blind, deaf, and mute. Members of the second group teach the first a prescribed sequence of gestures and motions. It is crucial to the experience that the first group are not aware of what the second group will be doing with them.

Once the class is divided into two groups, give the members of the first group blindfolds and ask them to sit in chairs placed in different parts of the room. Further instruct them to role play persons who cannot see, hear, or speak. The person role playing the handicapped individual has no idea what is going to take place.

After the first group has arranged chairs and blindfolds, take the second group aside and give them the following printed instructions:

Outlined below are a series of gestures and motions. Please teach your partner, who cannot see, hear, or speak, to do these movements in the order listed. You are finished when your partner can go through the entire sequence of movements on cue.

1. Nod head up and down.
2. Clench right fist.
3. Hold right hand on jaw.
4. Puff cheeks out.
5. Shake head back and forth.
6. Clasp hands together and hold them on the back of the head.
7. Stand up, turn around, and sit down.
8. Shake hands.

Once the task is completed, your partner may remove the blindfold. Remaining quiet and observing the others is important to the rest of the group.

Check to make sure the handout is clearly understood before the second group determines partners and begins the assignment.

A follow-up discusssion that might include such topics as teaching strategies, the role of the learner and the teacher, frustrations and successes, sensitivities, new awarenesses is vital to this activity.

Block Building

Outlined below are the instructions for a follow-up to "Mimics" that enable students to reverse the roles previously experienced. Give the following instructions to the first group.

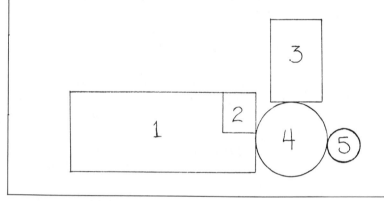

      Here are five different geometrically shaped blocks of wood. Outlined on this sheet is a top view, showing the blocks in a certain order. Please teach your partner, who is blindfolded, to place the pieces of wood so that they match the pattern outlined below. You and your partner must *not* talk to each other.
      You have finished when your partner can place the blocks in the right order without any help.

Once the students who are role playing the teachers have positioned themselves at tables and have received the sets of blocks and instruction sheets, the blindfolded students are led to the tables and seated. The sets of blocks used for this activity are easily made, though there are a variety of commercially manufactured children's blocks that can be used.

Square Off

The object of this challenge is for a group of blindfolded students (5 students per team) to work together and form a perfect square with 20 or 30 feet of rope. All of the rope must be used to make the square. Once the team feels they've completed the task, have them remove the blindfolds and observe the results.

      The fifth member of the team, who is not blindfolded, is responsible for passing out the rope and making sure it is not tangled. Though he or she may not assist the others to complete the challenge, he or she shares observations on how the group performed once the task is completed.

      Other geometric shapes can be used in this challenge.

Pretzel

This is a good icebreaker that gets students talking and working together to solve a group challenge. Have the class form circles with even numbers of people in each (8 or 10 for best results). Instruct the members of each circle to come together and clasp both hands of someone opposite them. Then each participant lets go of one hand and takes someone else's hand. The object of the challenge is to return to the circle without breaking the hand-to-hand contact.

Blazing a Trail

Divide students into small groups (4 or 5 per team). Give each group the assignment to lay a trail that another team will follow. Have each team select a subtle theme for its markers. These themes could include objects out of place (mushroom tied to a bush), scent, colors, categories of objects (seeds, wildflowers, trees). For instance, a scent trail could be made by crushing sprigs of mint and laying them on the ground or in bushes every 50 feet. The end of each trail is clearly marked with something that is to be brought back by the tracking team that is following the trail.

To maintain the challenge, the tracking team is not given the theme of the trail they are to follow. Rather, each team receives a list of all the themes and then is led to the general starting point of the trail they are to track. The team members scour the area to locate the beginning trail marker. Once something is found that matches one of the themes on the list, the group follows the trail.

Listed below are guidelines:

1. Trails should be about a quarter mile in length.
2. Trail markers should occur every 50 feet.
3. Trails cannot be located in close proximity to one another.
4. The tracking team should look for starting points in about a 50-foot square area.

Notes on the use of Sensitivity to the Environment activities:

Outdoor Language Adventures

"We learn if we have something in our hands."

Jean Piaget

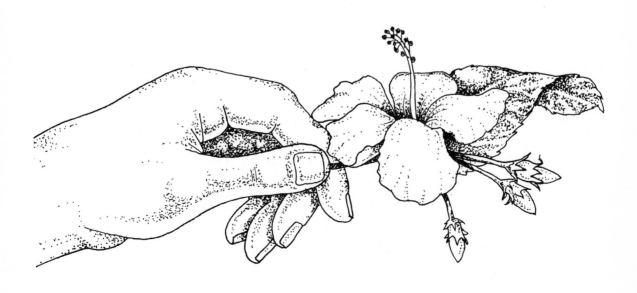

Every outdoor education experience can add to the development of language arts skills. Is there a better place than the out-of-doors to stimulate the senses and help communication with others? Poetry, writing stories, oral expression, and dramatics take on special meaning when sitting under a towering oak, walking through a sea of dandelions, or watching a bumble bee moving from flower to flower. The outdoors helps students become more receptive to everything around them by encouraging the use of their ears, noses, hands, and other parts of their bodies to channel sensory impressions. The natural environment is a persuasive beginning for learning and practicing the communication skills.

The child who has seen, heard, smelled, and felt the wonders of the unfolding earth in spring has a deep understanding of the word *spring*. If this child has experienced the movement of a grasshopper and frog, the ejection of seeds from a touch-me-not, or the bubbling from a natural spring, there are new meanings for the word and a different basis of comparison.

In language arts activities, have the students compare their descriptions of sights, sounds, and meanings. Help them note and appreciate words or phrases that are especially effective in conveying impressions and feelings. These skills enable students to transmit their thoughts and feelings, a large step in influencing the ideas and attitudes of other people.

The opportunity to awaken the child's senses is just outside the classroom door, a whole world of sensations waiting to tickle and tantalize, to spark the imagination, and to cause wonder. At the same time, the outdoors can be a vehicle to teach all language arts skills. Open the door to these experiences by trying the following activities. Others have found them useful; you will, too.

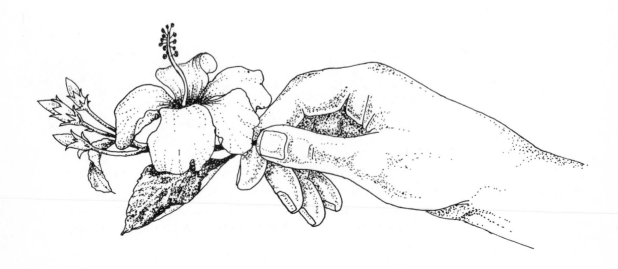

Telescope Adventuring

Purpose

To develop vocabulary, to practice descriptive writing skills while working with adverbs and adjectives, and to heighten sensory experiences.

Description

Observe objects in or near a pond, meadow, and woods through a cardboard telescope and communicate feelings and ideas about them. Photos taken with self-developing film can add another dimension to this activity if desired.

Materials

Pencil, spiral notebook, cardboard roll, camera that uses self-developing film (optional).

Process

Have the students look at objects in the pond, meadow, and edge of the woods through their cardboard rolls. Have them look at things at various angles rather than simply straight on.

If a camera is to be used, explain how to use it, and then allow each child to "look through" the camera lens (as they did with their cardboard rolls) at various angles and snap a picture.

During this time, students can also record in their spiral notebooks the various sights and sounds of nature, using adjectives and adverbs to describe the colors of fall, crispness of leaves on the ground, flocks of birds gathering for the journey south, squirrels gathering food for winter, or other season sensations.

Back in the classroom, have the students compose, using the list of adjectives and adverbs recorded in their notebooks, a short paragraph entitled "Open Up Your Eyes and Let the Sun Shine In."

Options and Extensions

Mount the photographs on tagboard and use them to tell a story or stimulate thinking for writing the descriptive paragraph. Have the students make up their own titles based on the pictures or on what they viewed through their cardboard telescope.

Simile Stroll

Purpose   To develop skill in writing similes, to enhance the ability to see relationships, and to expand communication skills.

Description   In a natural setting—school yard, stream, vacant lot—have students look for and complete comparisons such as the following:

> as rough as
> as smooth as
> as green as
> as velvet as

Materials   Pencil, small note pad, magnifying glass.

Process   Discuss what a simile is and its uses. Then experience a simile: Take a stroll and encourage students to look for relationships and express these comparisons as similes. Come together and share the writings. Read a few passages in literature where the author uses the simile technique.

Options and Extensions   A natural follow-up is to explore the use of metaphors by the same process described for similes. Some examples of metaphors might be: the root of the problem, a carpet of grass, or a blanket of snow.

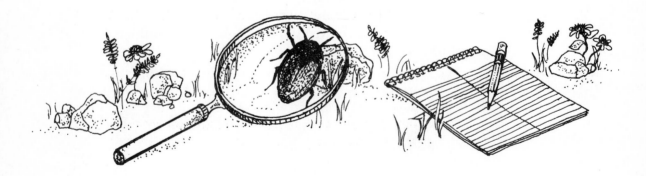

Who Am I?

Purpose   To review the observations of a hike or other outdoor experience, and to help students understand the purpose and nature of an interview while practicing oral and written communication skills.

Description   Students role-play a reporter and also natural objects that have been encountered during an outdoor experience. The reporters must utilize oral and written expressions while the "natural objects" will use oral description.

Materials   Pencil, spiral notebook.

Process   Use imaginary interviews to review the observations of an outdoor experience. These might take the form of one child who pretends to be a particular tree, bird, flower, insect, or rock. The reporter learns something about the life history of the natural objects being represented by asking what they have observed going on around them. Other questions might relate to changes expected in the future based on observations of the surroundings. The reporter writes up a story and titles it. Give each student an opportunity to role-play both parts.

Help the group identify the elements of a good interview, including purpose and nature, how one should be initiated, what kinds of questions to ask, how much time should be used, and proper closure. Interviewing methods can be introduced by this activity or be taught before the experience and practiced in the field.

Options and Extensions   Assign students more specific roles, so that one student asks questions, another records information, while a third investigates the surroundings for other evidence. Acting out and using nonverbal messages so that reporters must interpret the facts and evidence adds another dimension to "Who Am I?"

Me Tree

Purpose
To expand written expression, to enhance self-concept, to develop classifying and organizational skills, to develop the ability to see relationships, and to enhance communication skills.

Description
Students identify their physical and mental characteristics (large, angular, observant, sensitive), personality (outgoing, friendly), interests (fishing), and background (lots of accidents) and then select trees that generally reflect their traits.

Materials
Paper, pencil, clipboard, masking tape.

Process
Have each student take time to reflect on his or her physical qualities, personality traits, interests, and experiences, recording the highlights of these reflections. Next, have students explore a wooded setting and select trees that possess characteristics of their qualities. The students develop a narrative that illustrates these parallels. Finally, have them share their writings and trees with each other.

Options and Extensions
Expand the "Me Tree" to include characteristics from history, such as famous personality trees and biography trees.

Questioning a Spruce

Purpose   To develop written expression, to enhance creativity in thought, to practice paragraph development, to expand communication skills, and to develop positive feelings for the natural world.

Description   Students select trees and write up an interview based on observations, inferences, and interpretations of the tree's condition and setting.

Materials   Masking tape, clipboard, paper, pencil.

Process   Have students choose partners and select trees within a confined area. Mark the trees with masking tape while the teams record information relating to the tree's shape, size, texture, condition, and environment. Have students write up their interviews and then exchange descriptions. The teams visit the marked trees and attempt to match up the interviews with the trees. Follow up by sharing the writings with the whole group.

Options and Extensions   Establish tree interview stations on the school grounds: In this activity the teacher hands out "interviews" to students and asks them to identify particular marked trees.

A Poem Lovely as a Tree

Purpose
To develop creativity, to encourage poetic expression, to promote group awareness, and to heighten the sense of wonder for the outdoors.

Description
Teams of students focus on natural settings and objects from different vantage points, record their feelings and thoughts, and then express their thoughts in poetic verse as a group.

Materials
Clipboard, pencil, paper.

Process
Divide the class into teams of five or six students. Have each group select a scribe and choose an object or setting. Have team members place themselves at various vantage points and view quietly what they have selected. Have the recorder ask each student for a word or phrase that best describes his or her feelings about the object. The team works together to create a poem with the words and phrases and any necessary linking words. Visit the sites and have the teams share their poems with each other.

Options and Extensions
Have the groups write their poems on large sheets of chart paper and display them in school.

Hanger Put-Down

Purpose

To write descriptive paragraphs in an outdoor setting, to develop and expand vocabulary, to explore fantasy, and to heighten the awareness of the natural world.

Description

In a natural setting—forest, meadow, playground, beach, school yard—students focus on a very small segment of the selected environment and write a descriptive paragraph on one particular element within the chosen setting.

Materials

Hand lens, wire coat hanger, paper, pencil.

Process

Have each student take a hanger, hand lens, paper, and pencil and settle in a comfortable, interesting spot. The hanger should be stretched slightly and placed on the ground. For a period of time, have each student examine the environment within the boundary of the hanger. The observer selects something interesting and writes a short, descriptive paragraph. The hand lens may be used to provide new, different perspectives.

Have students leave the paragraphs beside the hanger and come together again, pair off, and visit each other's microenvironment. Have the visiting partner read the description and then try to identify what it is focused on.

Options and Extensions

Incorporate elements of fantasy into the activity by allowing the students to expand on their descriptions to include some creative fantasy—gnomes and hobbits, for example.

Who Was That Leaf I Saw You With?

Purpose
To practice writing descriptive paragraphs, to develop vocabulary, to identify qualities of a good description, and to heighten the awareness of the natural world.

Description
Students select a leaf and write a short descriptive paragraph about it.

Materials
Wide selection of leaves in triplicate, pencil, slips of paper (different kinds of plant stems and blossoms could be used as well).

Process
Divide group evenly among three tables. The following items should be on the tables: slips of paper, a pencil for each student, and two or three more leaves than there are students. Each person selects a leaf and writes a short descriptive paragraph about it. Afterward the groups switch tables and leaves. Then each team of students matches the descriptions with the leaves.

Follow-up discussion might include a comparison of the descriptions, identification of the qualities in a good description, why good descriptions are important, and reasons for the variations in the descriptions.

Options and Extensions
Use the leaf descriptions as a preliminary activity to some tree identification. Locate the trees on the school ground and match up the leaves. Mark the trees and have the students write stories about the changes through the seasons of the year.

Two By Two

Purpose   To help build vocabulary, to clearly identify the features of objects, to help students develop the process skills of observation and classification.

Description   Students are given a set of natural objects to observe and describe. They classify these as a group and construct a dichotomous key until all specimens have been separated singularly.

Materials   Chart paper, six different kinds of leaves (other natural objects such as rocks, flowers, stems, and twigs can be used), felt-tip pen.

Process   Divide students into groups of five or six and give them similar sets of natural objects (leaves work well as a beginning in dichotomous charting). This activity can be done at tables if they are available or on the floor. Spread out the chart paper within the circle of students or in front of them. Have students follow the steps below.

1. From the specimens selected, have the students take one and examine it for several minutes, looking for observable characteristics.
2. Have students discuss the observed characteristics with each other. (Some discussions on observable characteristics rather than inferences might be helpful at this point.)
3. All specimens should be put into two sets based on major likenesses and differences of observable characteristics. (The word *dichotomy*—"division into two parts, groups, or classes"—is the key to this activity.)
4. Have students individually discuss the criteria used to separate specimens and then construct a dichotomous key until all specimens have been separated singularly, as shown on the next page.

   Note: Encourage positive descriptions to help build vocabulary and more clearly identify the individual features of an object.
       For example, use

   thick/thin instead of thick/not thick
   sharp/blunt instead of sharp/not sharp
   round/oval instead of round/not round

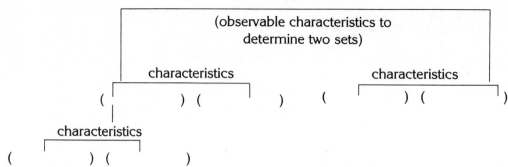

Five Specimens

(observable characteristics to
determine two sets)

characteristics   characteristics

(   ) (   )   (   ) (   )

characteristics

(   ) (   )

5. Give each group the sixth object of their set so that they can now place it into the classification system they have developed.

6. Each group should now select one sample and use the words in the key to describe that sample to other groups. As this is done, each group can hold up the object they feel has been described until all six are identified.

Options and Extensions

One or more samples can be selected and the class can use the words to write a description of it in sentence form. Instead of leaves, the students in the class can be classified by observable characteristics in a dichotomous key. Primary teachers might consider modifying this activity by using two or three specimens.

Poetry Paths

Purpose   To explore creative expression, to develop word relations, to understand parts of speech, and to experience poetic techniques.

Description   Students explore the out-of-doors and develop poetic techniques through the use of cinquain and nouning poems.

Materials   Hand lens, paper, pencil, sample format sheet of cinquain and nouning technique, clipboard.

Process   Have each student select a comfortable setting, view surroundings and eventually focus on an object or aspect of the environment—mossy bank, ravine, bumble bee. Use the cinquain and nouning models to create descriptions of the selected items. Assemble the class and have students share their poems.
Format models and examples of cinquain and nouning:

Cinquain
Title in two syllables
Description of title in
    four syllables
Action in six syllables
Expression of feeling in
    eight syllables
Another word for the title in
    two syllables

Flower
Yellow, brightness
Pop up everywhere now
Reaching out to the honey bee
Fragrant

Nouning
Noun title
Two adjectives
Three verbs
Phrase
Repeat noun

Honey Bee
Silent, rapid
Flies, looks, feeds
Busy in her work
Honey bee

Options and Extensions   Have the students write one-sentence descriptions of simple things they observed. Stress using personal experience for comparison so that the descriptions are more vivid and meaningful.

Nature on the Line

Purpose

To develop word relations, to expand vocabulary, to further enhance communication skills, and to practice classification techniques.

Description

Students use word matrixes to explore natural environments; objects are observed and classified in the matrixes.

Materials

Clipboard, word matrix sheet, sample list of word categories, pencil.

Process

Ask students to select words from word categories and set up the matrix sheets. Have the class explore a natural setting and classify objects that match the word pairs on the matrix to fill in the spaces. Example of a word matrix:

Texture

	Slick	Hard	Velvety	Rough	Hairy
Red					
Green					
Blue					
Brown					

Color

Examples of word categories:

Shape	Density	Size	Temperature
lobed	lumpy	bulky	clammy
billowy	solid	miniature	dry
pointed	porous	short	moist
oval	spongy	large	cool

Options and Extensions

Primary teachers might want to use egg cartons or boxes for their matrices and actually have students collect the items.

Clothesline Composition

Purpose
To explore creative expression, to develop word relations, to understand parts of speech, and to experience poetic techniques.

Description
Students explore the outdoors and develop poetic techniques through the use of cinquain, haiku, and nouning poems.

Materials
11″ × 8″ tagboard picture frame (1″ wide), clipboard, pencil, sample format sheet, cord, clothespins.

Process
Stretch a clothesline between two or three trees *at eye level.* Give students tagboard picture frames and clothespins. Have each student walk along the rope and pin up the frame at random.

Once a particular positioning of the frame is selected, have each student choose a poetic form and write about the view through the frame. Attach the finished poem next to the frame. Finally, have students view each other's work.

Note: cinquain and nouning were described in "Poetry Paths." *Haiku* is a Japanese verse form that has three unrhymed lines of 5, 7, and 5 syllables.

Options and Extensions
Substitute clothes hangers for the tagboard picture frames. Use a short, descriptive paragraph or several sentences instead of poetic composition.

Notes on the use of Outdoor Language Adventures:

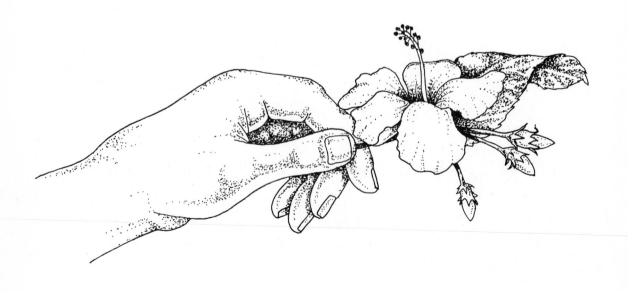

Schoolyard
Math
Investigations

"I think that I shall never see
a numeral as pretty as a three."

B. Ucki

There are many learning situations in mathematics where outdoor education activities may supplement classroom teaching. Some of the basic concepts included in the mathematics program of an elementary or junior high school are counting, measurement, averaging, estimation, ratio, proportion, geometric shapes, and problem solving. All of these concepts can be introduced, taught, and reinforced in the outdoor classroom.

As students intellectually mature, a certain internal consistency develops within their environment. This is the essential foundation for the teaching of mathematics and whole number concepts. The understanding of the abstract idea of numbers is preceded by an ordering of the physical attributes of the world. Things that are more immediately measureable than numbers include any property that the student is able to compare by touching, smelling, seeing, hearing, or tasting.

The activities presented in this chapter help students generalize information gained from their experience and move from the concept of whole numbers to ordering and classification to ratio, proportion, and problem solving.

An activity such as measuring the blue whale or a tyrannosaurus rex out on the playground is a concrete experience that gives meaning to a variety of concepts, including size, estimation, distance, and units of measure. Making a half-acre come to life on a school football or soccer field is a natural extension of the students' perceptions of their physical environment.

Additionally, the concepts of similar triangles and the isosceles right triangle are given direct application in the activities dealing with inaccessible distances. No longer is a theorem alive only in the geometry section of a math book; it is now being used to determine the height of a flag pole or a tree on the school grounds. In this way, mathematics in the out-of-doors is a valuable aid in practicing computation skills, extending concepts previously introduced, and motivating the students.

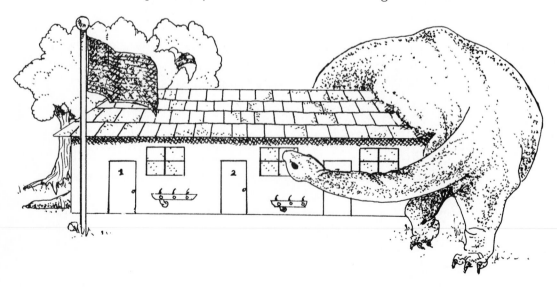

Hike for Counters

Purpose   To collect sets of counters that may be used in daily number work.

Description   Students look for natural counters, such as pebbles, twigs, acorn caps, nuts, and so on, in various outdoor settings—school yard, park, stream, beach, or forest.

Materials   Small plastic bag with draw string or other closed container.

Process   Talk with children about the kinds of natural objects that would make good counters. Discuss which of these objects would most likely be found in the environment to be visited. Let each student choose the object he or she wishes to collect. Provide them with a small container to hold their counters. After the hike have students share their collections, talk about the number of objects needed in a set, and select the best items to keep for counters.

 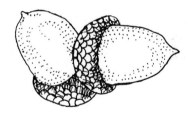

Options and Extensions   Introduce the abacus and discuss how counters are used. Small children will enjoy using their counters to count items around the school, such as toadstools, trees, or doorknobs.

A High, Low, Fat Hike

Purpose

To clarify certain words and their comparative forms: high, higher, highest; low, lower, lowest; fat, fatter, fattest; to express differences in heights, weights, and distances in these terms; to practice estimating.

Description

Students select specific words and their comparative forms: high, low, light, heavy, near, far, short, and so on. They select and collect natural objects that correctly illustrate the term and its comparative form.

Materials

3 × 5 index cards.

Process

Brainstorm with the class and compile a list of words used in comparative measurement. Discuss the concept of comparative forms and get the class to identify the comparative forms for the words listed. Have the students pair off and write one or two words and their comparative forms on blank cards. Each team is then responsible for collecting samples of objects that will illustrate their words and comparative forms. After the hike, have students come together and share their findings. Use flash cards for further drill.

Options and Extensions

Branch out from terms used in simple measurement and identify some general words: spongy, dry, lumpy, cool, velvety, and so on, and their comparative forms. Plan a hike to a nearby outdoor setting; locate objects that characterize their words and their comparative forms.

Count a Thousand Walk

Purpose
To understand the meaning of large numbers, to practice counting and estimating, and to experience a problem-solving process.

Description
Students count a thousand of something and prove that they did it.

Materials
Pencil, small notebook or clipboard, paper.

Process
Take the class to an outdoor setting and give them the assignment to count a thousand of something. What they count and how they do it are decisions each student makes. Encourage the students to develop their own understandings of and solutions to the problem. Come together after a short time and allow the class to share their interpretations of the problem and give proof that they completed the task.

Options and Extensions
Assign the class other large numbers to count: 10,000; 100,000; 1,000,000. Have students compare approaches.

Pace and Space

Purpose

To determine length of a pace, to develop computation skills, and to practice averaging.

Description

Students establish length of a pace by counting their steps over a hundred-foot course. The course is stepped off and the number of paces is determined. This number is divided into 100 to calculate length of a pace.

Materials

100-foot tape measure, note pad, pencil.

Process

Mark off a hundred-foot course in an open, flat field or on a sidewalk near the school. Discuss why it is important to use a normal pace when counting steps along the course. Have students pace off the course four times and find their average number of steps. Encourage the class to determine what the next step would be to calculate size of a pace. Have the students round off their paces to the nearest half foot. Most paces will be 2, 2½, or 3 feet in length. Use the pace method to determine various distances around the school.

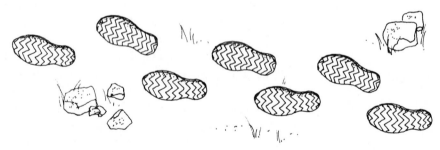

Options and Extensions

Have students estimate the distance from the school to their homes and then pace off the route to determine the actual distance. Make a table or graph of the measurements determined.

A Dinosaur in the Parking Lot?

Purpose
To interpret size by demonstrating the dimensions of large objects; to practice measurement using the pace method, yard stick, or measuring wheel.

Description
To demonstrate the relative size of famous prehistoric reptiles, students plot their dimensions on open space around the school yard.

Materials
Marking stakes, yard sticks, or meter sticks.

Process
Discuss with the class the size of some large reptiles of prehistoric times. This could be done after reading a story or book about dinosaurs. Ask them to estimate how large some of the animals mentioned in the story were. If the story does not tell the size (length will do) of a tyrannosaurus rex or a brontosaurus, help the students look up this information in an encyclopedia.

Divide the class into small groups and have them pick one of their favorite dinosaurs. Take the class out on the playground or field and have each group measure the length of the animal they chose using the pacing method described in the previous lesson.

It is a good idea to use several stakes or markers so that the class can compare the different lengths of the animals. Stakes with colored ribbon or crepe paper tied around the top help identify the distance measured. You may want to measure the distance using a yard stick, meter stick, or measuring wheel and compare the results with the pacing method.

Options and Extensions
Other stories can provide examples of different-sized animals and objects for the students to measure and compare. The blue whale, a rocket for an earth satellite, or the ocean-going ships Columbus sailed are other objects to compare and contrast.

Mathematics

Geometric Pattern Search

Purpose

To review geometric shapes; to visualize the relationship between squares, rectangles, and triangles; and to relate geometric shapes to the outside world.

Description

Small groups of students work together with a variety of geometric shapes that when arranged correctly will make five squares of equal size. This activity is followed by a hike, during which the students try to identify objects outdoors that are similar in shape to the geometric patterns used to form the squares.

Materials

Six packets containing five squares and the geometric shapes used to make each of the squares (see page 7 in Chapter 1 for directions on making squares).

Process

Divide the class into small groups of four or five students. Give each group a packet of geometric shapes and have them work together to arrange all the geometric shapes so that they form five squares of equal size. Doing this activity nonverbally ensures maximum group participation. After the groups have finished, let students identify the various shapes used to make the squares and discuss the strategies used to complete the task. Encourage the class to identify things they might find in the school yard that are similar to the shapes used to form the squares. Have each student select one or two of the geometric shapes in the packets and search the school grounds for natural or man-made objects with the same shape. Come together and share findings.

Options and Extensions

Identify other environments the students could visit: city and residential streets, park, and cemetery; go on a pattern search to these areas with the class.

Going Around in Circles

Purpose

To reinforce mathematical concepts of diameter and circumference of a circle while comparing tree sizes around the school yard.

Description

Students find the diameter of tree given the circumference and the formula c = dπ. The students then record the relationship between the diameter and circumference of a tree using a broken line graph.

Materials

Worksheet, metric/English tape measure, pencil.

Process

Have the students work in pairs. Give each pair a tape measure and worksheet. Label ten trees in the school yard (1–10) by putting masking tape completely around each trunk. Have one student in the pair measure the circumference of the tree by putting the tape measure over the masking tape while the other student records the data. Once the trees are measured, each pair must compute the diameter of the tree at the point of the masking tape, using c = dπ and π = 3.14. Have students record the results on a broken line graph.

Options and Extensions

Use a lesson in estimation as a follow-up activity. Ask each pair of students to estimate the number of leaves on the tree. Discussion: (1) What is an estimate? and (2) Where and how can estimates be used? Students may be asked to guess the number of leaves first and then use a systematic technique, such as counting the number of leaves on a branch or two as close to the ground as possible and then counting the number of branches and multiplying to arrive at an estimate. Then compare results.

Diameter and Circumference of a Tree

Tree	Circumference	Diameter
1		
2		
3		
4		
5		
6		
7		
8		
9		
10		

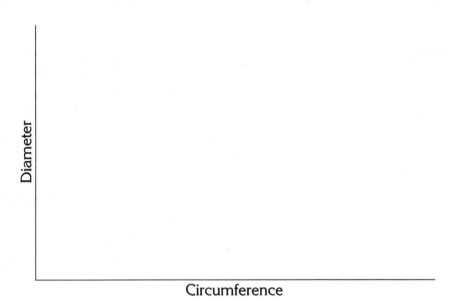

Diameter

Circumference

Chapter 3   Schoolyard Math Investigations

Making a Half-Acre Come to Life

Purpose

To develop skills in measuring area, to experience practical applications of measurement, and to learn about the use of scale models.

Description

Teams of students are assigned the task of staking out a half-acre on the playground using various geometric shapes. In addition to the outdoor assignment, the students develop scale drawings of their half-acres. The half-acre plots staked out on the school yard provide a concrete feeling for a half-acre; the scale models project a graphic view of a half-acre's many variations in shape.

Materials

Clipboard, paper, pencil, tape measure, ruler, flugel stakes, hammer.

Process

Discuss the concept of an acre, its size, use, and variation in shape. Organize the class into small teams and have them survey and stake out a half-acre on the playground and draw up a scale model of the plot. Suggested scale: 1″ = 24′. Work with the groups to identify guidelines for the assignment, including the shape of the plot, materials needed, correct formula, and work assignments. The following information is needed:

Area Formulas for Geometric Shapes

One Acre = 43,560 square feet
1/2 Acre = 21,780 square feet

Area of a square or rectangle = length × width
Area of a circle = πr^2

$$\pi = 3.14 \text{ or } 22/7$$

$$r = \text{radius}$$

Area of a triangle = 1/2 base × height

Each team decides what geometric shape to use and the desired dimensions. For example, if the half-acre is a rectangle, the group may decide to have a width of 100 ft. The team substitutes 100 ft. for the width in the formula and determines the length as follows:

$$\text{Area} = \text{length} \times \text{width}$$

$$21{,}780\,\text{ft.} = \text{length} \times 100\,\text{ft.}$$

$$\frac{21{,}780\,\text{ft.}}{100\,\text{ft.}} = \text{length}$$

$$217.8\,\text{ft.} = \text{length}$$

Visit the different plots with the class and display the scale models of these plots.

Options and Extensions

Land use management, surveying, zoning, taxation, and city planning are a few interesting spin-off issues you may want to discuss and research further with your class.

Brim of the Hat

Purpose   To provide students with a simple, accurate technique for estimating inaccessible distances.

Description   Students use the brim of a hat or the palm of the hand above the eyes as a sighting guide for measuring inaccessible distances. They transfer the distance that cannot be measured to an area that can be measured and then use conventional measuring methods for their determinations.

Materials   A hat or cap with a brim, measuring devices such as a yard stick or tape.

Process   Discuss the Brim of the Hat estimating method with the class and identify the situations under which this technique could be used. Mark off a number of distances on the playground and have small teams of students estimate these distances. The following steps are used in the Brim of the Hat method:

1. Sight under the brim of the hat or the edge of the palm to the opposite bank of river (or points designated on the playground), raising or lowering the head until a proper line of sight is established (figure 1).
2. Without moving the head, turn slowly at right angles to the river and line up the brim or edge of palm with the base of some landmark (figure 2).
3. Pace off the distance from where you stand to the sighted landmark. This distance will approximate the width of the river (figure 3).
4. Convert the number of paces into feet or yards.

Sight
Figure 1

Turn right or left
Figure 2

Pace off
Figure 3

Let teams check their estimations with the actual measurement. Plan a field trip to sites where this technique can be applied, such as a nearby pond, river, or stream.

Options and Extensions

Encourage students to research the Brim of the Hat technique and identify examples in early military history where this form of estimating was used.

Isosceles Option, On Two

Purpose
To estimate inaccessible distances using the principle of an isosceles right triangle.

Description
Compasses are used to establish an isosceles right triangle over an inaccessible distance (or a simulated one). (Refer to Chapter 5, "Lost and Found," to learn how to determine a bearing.) The length of the accessible side of the isosceles right triangle is measured in order to estimate the inaccessible side. Thus, two sides of the isosceles right triangle are equal in length and the two angles formed by the sides and the hypotenuse are 45°.

Materials
Silva® compass, paper, pencil, wooden stakes, hammer.

Process
Discuss with students the characteristics of an isosceles right triangle. Mark off several distances on the playground with wooden stakes or markers and have small groups of students estimate these distances using the following steps:

1. Use the compass to determine bearing from Point A to Point B on opposite bank of a river (or points designated on the playground).
2. Find bearing from Point A to Point B (180° is used in the example).
3. Take a new reading from A by subtracting 90° to form line x (if bearing from A to B is 180°, line x is in the direction of 90°).

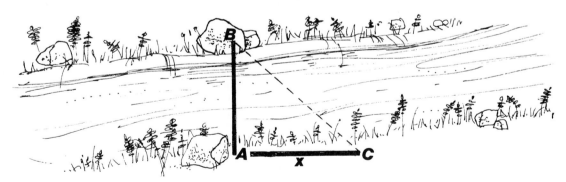

4. Move along line x to a point C where the bearing from point C to point B is 225° (180° + 45°). This forms an isosceles right triangle ABC with sides AB = AC.

5. Pace off distance between Point A and Point C to determine the width of the stream at AB.

Have students check answers with the actual measurements. You may want to plan a field trip to a location where this technique can actually be applied. Compare this technique with the Brim of the Hat method.

Options and Extensions

Invite a surveyor to visit the class, demonstrate the equipment, and explain techniques used to determine inaccessible distances.

Bank to Bank

Purpose

To provide practical experience using the principles of similar triangles, and to practice estimating distances.

Description

Similar triangles are established to estimate inaccessible distances. In similar triangles, the angles are the same and the sides of the triangles are in exact proportion to each other.

Materials

Three stakes, hammer, paper, pencil.

Process

Discuss the characteristics of similar triangles. Mark off several distances on the playground and assign small groups of students to estimate these distances using the following procedure:

1. Have students identify point A, a large object (tree, rock, pole) on the other side of a river (or points designated on the playground).
2. Place a marker, Point B, on the bank exactly opposite Point A.
3. At right angles to AB, pace off along the bank for 50 feet to Point C and place a marker.
4. Continue pacing along the river's edge in the same line for another 25 feet (1/2 of BC); at this spot place a marker, point D.
5. At D, turn away from the river at a right angle to line DB and walk to a point where marker C is in a straight line with point A and stop. This is point E. DE is half the length of AB. Pace off this distance and double it to determine the full distance across the river at AB.

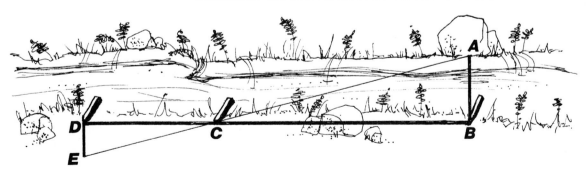

Options and Extensions

Provide an opportunity for the students to compare the Similar Triangles method with the Brim of the Hat and Isosceles Right Triangle methods.

The Shadow Knows

Purpose
To provide practical application of the concept of ratios, to estimate heights, and to work on measurement and computation skills.

Description
Estimating the height of an unknown object by comparing its shadow to the height of an object already measured.

Material
Meter or yard stick, paper, pencil, tape measure (optional).

Process
Review concepts of ratio and proportion and then identify situations where estimating the height of an object is needed. Select a variety of tall objects on the playground—flag pole, trees, goal posts, buildings—and have students use the following steps to estimate their heights:

1. Measure the shadow of a tree or other tall object (see illustration). This may be done with a tape measure or by pacing.
2. Place a yard or meter stick in a vertical position on the same slope as the tree and measure the stick's shadow. The lengths of the two sides of the triangle formed by the stick and its shadow, XYZ, are thus known and in proportion to the sides of the triangle ABC made by the tree and its shadow.

Set up a ratio or proportion problem and work it out: XY/AB = YZ/BC.

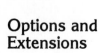

Options and Extensions
Invite a forester to come to class and discuss the techniques used to estimate the height of trees and to determine board feet.

Stake Out

Purpose

To experience practical application of the principles of similar triangles, to practice estimating height, and to develop computation skills.

Description

Similar triangles are established to estimate heights. In similar triangles, the angles are the same and the sides of the triangles are in exact proportion to each other.

Materials

Meter or yard stick, paper, pencil, tape measure (optional).

Process

Review the characteristics of similar triangles. Select a number of tall objects on the school yard and have pairs of students use the concept of similar triangles to estimate the heights of objects in the following manner:

1. Stake or hold the meter or yard stick on the ground in upright position (h) and have a second person lie down at Point A and sight with his or her eye close to the ground so that the top of the stick is in line with the top of the object being measured (C) (see illustration). Establish similar triangles ADE and ABC and set up a proportion problem: $AD/h = AB/H$.

2. Measure the distances AD and AB and set up the proportion problem to determine H, the height of the tree.

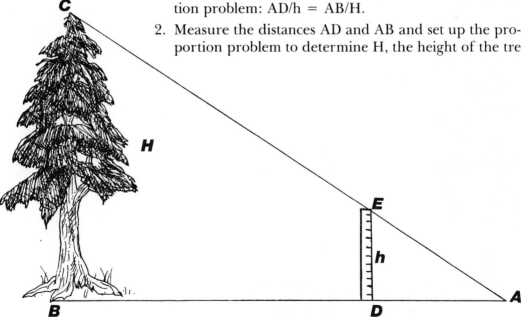

Options and Extensions

Relate this concept to plane geometry and discuss some of the theorems dealing with similar triangles.

The Only Way Is Up

Purpose
To estimate height using the concept of an isosceles right triangle.

Description
A clinometer (vertical protractor) is used to establish an isosceles right triangle, one side of which represents an unknown height.

Materials
Clinometer (wood, tacks, heavy cardboard, string, weight; see directions for making it below), paper, pencil, tape measure (optional).

Process
Go over the characteristics of an isosceles right triangle. Select several tall objects on the school yard and have pairs of students use the clinometer to estimate the object's height in the following manner:

1. Students use a clinometer and move toward or away from the objects being measured until an imaginary line from the student's eye to the top of the object forms a 45° angle (see illustration). Since the two sides in an isosceles right triangle are equal, Side A is equal to Side B in the figure.

2. Students measure the distance from where they are to the object by pacing or using a tape and add their height at eye level to determine the height of the object.

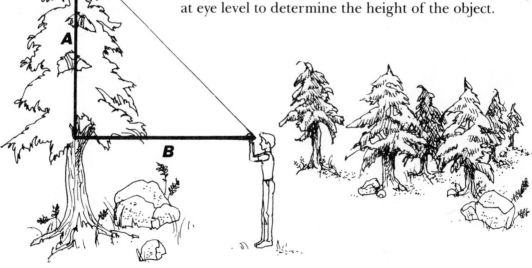

Compare the students' findings with the actual measurement. Discuss the merits of all the techniques for estimating heights and review possible reasons for the variation in answers.

Making the Clinometer

1. Use a straight piece of wood 8 to 10 inches long for a support.
2. Cut a half circle of heavy cardboard.
3. Use a protractor to add degree marks to the cardboard, marking zero at the point that is exactly perpendicular to the wood support.
4. Tack the cardboard to the center of the wood, making sure the top is parallel to the wooden straight edge.
5. Place a tack exactly in the center of the top of the cardboard.
6. Attach a weight to a string and suspend the string from the tack.

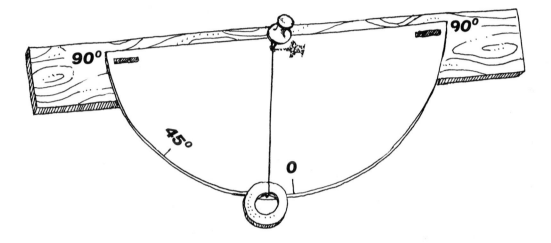

Options and Extensions

Have the students make isosceles right triangles out of heavy contact paper or cardboard. Use these in place of the clinometer to estimate heights.

Notes on the use of School Yard Math Investigations:

Art Experiences in Nature

"Art is a form of supremely delicate awareness . . .
the state of being one with the object."

D. H. Lawrence

Natural arts and crafts provides an important avenue for developing awareness, stimulating the imagination, sharpening the senses, and providing a form for expression of ideas. Every season presents new beauty and different opportunities for experiencing the out-of-doors.

Students use leaves, flowers, cobwebs and other natural materials in activities such as "The Big Squeeze," "Flowers Forever," and "Cobweb Copies" to preserve the beauty of nature and appreciate it a little longer.*

"Be a Tree" and "Weaving Adventure" encourage students to use new forms of expression. Other activities such as "Hue Hike," "Rub It Out," and "Bits and Pieces" enable students to use a combination of common materials to inspire them to create with their own hands.

Natural handicraft is an area of recreation and learning that lends itself to a variety of activities for students of all ages. It is easily incorporated into any educational curriculum or setting. Students exposed to these ideas will not only enjoy the learning experience now but will continue it as a hobby and form of relaxation.

Note to the teacher: Discretion is important in using natural materials. Collecting of leaves and flowers should be minimized. When in doubt as to whether to collect, have the students bring flowers from a home garden or provide specimens yourself.

Do You Remember?

Purpose

To increase awareness of objects that are so much a part of the students' lives, to improve memory through visual contact.

Description

This project involves drawing objects from memory after a conscious effort has been made to increase awareness and recall details.

Materials

Paper and something to use for drawing.

Process

Select something familiar near the school for the students to recall. Ask the students questions about this building, tree, or park that will begin to create an awareness for characteristics and details.

Take the students to observe the object or place you've selected with the idea that they need to remember as many characteristics and details as they possibly can.

Return to the classroom and have students do sketches from memory. Help them recall details about the area and surroundings. Students should do the sketches in only one color in order to focus on details. They may want to add more color later on, but the monochromatic sketches will be very striking.

Options and Extensions

This project can also be done using familiar objects collected by students, including leaves, rocks, pine cones, shells, nuts, and so on. Display sketches with the actual objects.

Art

Be a Tree

Purpose To develop a sense of aesthetic appreciation through participation and to encourage imagination through dramatization and painting.

Description After dramatizing the lives of trees, students paint pictures of them.

Materials Tempera paints, brushes, large construction paper.

Process Have students identify characteristics of trees. Visit trees in a back yard, in an orchard, in a park, or in the school yard.

Have the students do tree dramatizations, using their arms as the branches and their legs as the trunk. How does the tree look during a storm? How does a fruit tree look in the spring? How does a young tree look in comparison with an old tree? What would happen to change the tree in different kinds of weather or during the different seasons?

After feeling what it might be like to be a tree, have the students paint pictures of them.

Options and Extensions This project can be done in any season. Tree pictures can be saved from many seasons to use for Arbor Day activities. Students might choose specific trees to paint different portraits all through the seasons.

Hue Hike

Purpose   To increase awareness of the variety of coloration in nature.

Description   Students do an inventory of natural colors in the out-of-doors.

Materials   Paper, pencils, plastic bags.

Process   Discuss color variations readily noticeable in the classroom.
Name several variations of colors (red, crimson, scarlet).
　　Have students list different colors on paper and divide into
groups and go find examples in nature.
　　Have students write down where they found examples of
different colors.
　　Compile a master list of objects found on individual
inventories.

Options and   This project takes on an interesting twist when each group is
Extensions   given a single color. Students will be surprised at the wide variety of shades and tints of single colors. These colors may require
much more creative labeling.

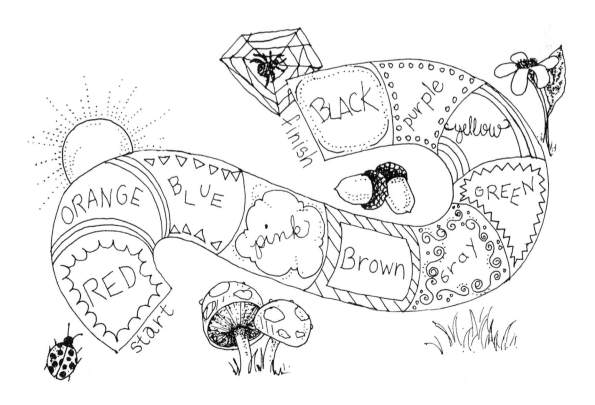

Bits and Pieces

Purpose
To familiarize students with some of the techniques and principles used in making mosaics and to combine several small objects to create an original natural mosaic.

Description
Students use natural materials they have collected to make mosaics. Be sure they do not pick or uproot any plants.

Materials
Small natural objects such as pebbles, beans, tiny shells, seeds; white glue; cardboard; piece of wood or matt board; acrylic spray.

Process
Have students spread white glue across the surface of a piece of cardboard.

Using the tiny objects, have them create a design, gluing the objects very close together. The designs might be done by starting in the corners and working in, by starting at the center and working out, by making stripes, or by making various other patterns. The design can be enhanced through color and size variations.

After the objects have been glued to cover the entire piece of cardboard, the mosaic can be sprayed with acrylic spray to preserve and protect the natural materials.

Options and Extensions
This project can also be done using familiar objects collected by students, including leaves, rocks, pine cones, shells, nuts, and so on. Display sketches with the actual objects.

Flowers Forever

Purpose   To preserve flowers for collections, future study, and decoration.

Description   Flowers are dried and preserved using the sand-dried method.

Materials   Cardboard box, silica sand, scissors, fresh-picked flowers, florist tape, and wire.

Process   Emphasize with your students the importance of picking only a limited number of flowers and leaves. You may also wish to point out specific specimens to collect or provide these natural objects yourself.

Have students fill their cardboard boxes (a shoe box works well) half full of sand and cut the stem of the flower down to about 3 inches. Then have them push the stem of each flower into the sand.

Have students gradually sprinkle the sand over the flower until it is completely covered. If flowers are thick with many petals, like roses, open the petals slightly and fill in the spaces between the petals with sand. Place the box in a dry location. Let the flowers dry in the sand for at least two weeks.

Check the flowers after two weeks. When the flowers have dried, carefully tilt the box and pour out the sand; lift out the flowers. Have students slide a wire up the center of each stem into the flower and secure it with florist tape. Use the flowers for studies, collections, and gifts.

Options and Extensions   Many microwave ovens include information on how to dry most common flowers in a matter of minutes.

The Big Squeeze

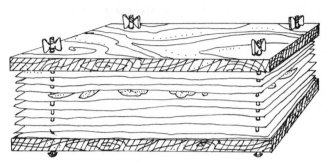

Purpose

To press and preserve flowers and leaves.

Description

Students will make presses and select various plants to preserve.

Materials

Two 12-inch squares of plywood (any size will work, as long as it is square or rectangular and at least eight inches wide at its narrowest point), drill, four wing nuts, four carriage bolts, paper punch, blotter paper.

Process

You may wish to point out specific specimens to collect or provide them yourself.

Drill a hole in each corner of both pieces of the wood. (Drill through both layers at the same time to ensure that the holes line up properly.) The holes should be about 1/2 inch from each edge. Have students cut blotter paper slightly smaller than the size of the wood. Mark the blotter paper for holes. Use a paper punch to make a hole in each corner of every sheet of blotter paper.

Have students slide the carriage bolts up through the bottom piece of wood. Place ten sheets of blotter paper and the top wooden piece on the bolts. Screw on the wing nuts.

When students are ready to press flowers or leaves, have them take the press apart and put the plant in the middle of the blotter paper layers. (The blotter paper absorbs the moisture from the plants.) Then have them replace the top wooden piece and screw the wing nuts down tightly.

Options and Extensions

Pressed leaves and flowers can be used for scientific specimens as well as for stationery or pictures. Dried, pressed leaves and flowers can be glued onto wood or slate with a mixture of one part water to one part white glue. Once the glue is dry, the arrangement can be sprayed with acrylic spray for preservation.

Sun Silhouettes

Purpose   To print natural objects using the sun.

Description   By using light sensitive paper and the sun, students make silhouette prints of natural objects.

Materials   Light sensitive blueprint paper (available from architectural supply stores), ammonia, large can (available from school kitchens), small dish, objects to print, clear plastic wrap.

Process   You may wish to point out specific specimens to collect or provide them yourself.

In a fairly dark area, have students arrange several flat, natural objects (leaves, flowers or feathers work well) on a piece of light sensitive paper. Place the paper on a piece of wood or cardboard. It is important to work quickly, so it is suggested that the design be planned out before beginning.

Cover the paper with a layer of plastic wrap so that the objects won't blow away. Take the wrapped paper into bright sunlight. Depending on how bright the sun is, students should expose the paper for between 30 seconds and 2 minutes.

Bring the paper inside and unwrap it. Place it inside a large can so that the print side faces the center of the can. Place the can upside down over a small dish of ammonia, and leave it for about five minutes. Check the print periodically. The print will gradually turn from light pink to darker shades of purple and blue. The areas where the objects were on the paper will remain white.

Mount the prints on tagboard or matt board and display out of the way of direct sunlight.

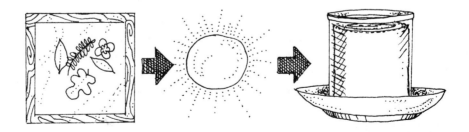

Options and Extensions   Have students make pin hole cameras and use them to take some pictures. Study how film is processed and visit a photography lab at the local high school.

Cobweb Copies

Purpose
To observe designs in nature, to record the delicacy of natural designs, and to find examples of natural symmetry.

Description
After a discovery walk for observation of symmetrical designs, web prints are made to record natural symmetry.

Materials
White drawing paper, spray paint, spider web.

Process
Have students search an area with considerable foliage for examples of symmetry. Take along a spray can of paint and some paper.

When students locate a web, hold the spray can about 18 inches away from it and spray quickly with a back and forth motion. The paint will look like tiny beads on the threads.

Carefully place a sheet of paper over the web, curving the paper so that it first touches the web's center and then gradually flattens out to the edges. Let the print dry completely after you pull it away from the web. Some of the web will remain in the print.

Options and Extensions
Other examples of symmetry include leaves, snowflakes, feathers, or flowers. Discuss with students other possibilities of symmetrical objects in nature. Take a school yard inventory of objects that are symmetrical. What are the different types of symmetry? How can these other symmetrical objects be recorded? Could students use strings to make their own webs?

Profiles in Color

Purpose
To familiarize students with easy printing techniques using paint and natural materials.

Description
Students collect objects and print them on paper.

Materials
Objects to print with—leaves, vegetables and fruit (cabbage, carrots, potatoes, apples, lettuce, peppers), fish, wood, bark; paint (tempera or watercolors); brushes; paper.

Process
Have students collect printing materials from gardens and other outdoor settings. Cut vegetables and fruit into slices, wedges, and so on.

Have students coat the bottom of the cut vegetables and fruit or other objects with paint—tempera works best for fruits and vegetables. Use watercolors on the back of a leaf for finely detailed prints.

Have students press each painted object onto paper and remove. A print will remain. The prints can be done singly or several can be combined for an interesting composition. Let each print dry and then have students sign their work.

Options and Extensions
When mounted on different colors of paper or matted, these prints make an attractive natural display. Have students try doing some prints on colored paper with white paint, or a contrasting color for interest. Let them try doing a print using more than one color.

Art

Rub It Out

Purpose

To record natural designs from nature for collections, displays, or decorations.

Description

Students create interesting design compositions by rubbing textures from natural objects onto paper.

Materials

Paper (shelf paper or thin drawing paper works well); crayons, pencils, or charcoal; objects to rub.

Process

Have students place leaves wrong side up on a flat surface. Then have them place a sheet of paper over the leaves and rub on the paper with a pencil or crayon (use the side of the crayon).

For interesting results, vary the crayon rubbings by having students rub all one direction with a light color and then rub in the opposite direction over the same area with a darker color. Try any number of different color combinations. These are really striking when mounted and can easily be done by even the youngest children.

Stump rubbings can also be interesting. Have students tape a large piece of paper over a tree stump and rub with the side of a crayon. These rubbings can be especially good for a discussion of a tree's age and growth. When did the tree grow fastest? What are some possible reasons for the tree being cut down? What historic events were taking place at the time this tree started to grow? Are there any signs of disease?

Options and Extensions

Students might want to write a history of a tree, including change in the tree's environment, possible reasons for the tree growing where it is, uses of the tree through the years, reasons for the tree falling or being cut down.

Wreathing Naturally

Purpose   To collect and use natural materials to create decorations.

Description   With a variety of natural materials, students make wreaths to be used for decorations and as a visual collection.

Materials   Pine cones (all sizes, shapes, varieties), pods, nuts, seeds, dried flowers, cardboard, linoleum adhesive, knife.

Process   Discuss types of pods, nuts and pine cones and where they can be found. Have students collect lots of pine cones, pods, and so on.

    Cut a shape from cardboard to use for a wreath. Cover the surface of the cardboard with linoleum adhesive.

    Have students start covering the wreath with the largest cones and pods, filling in the smaller spaces with nuts, pods, flowers, and small cones. Layer smaller objects to build up some height to the wreath. No cardboard should be showing when the arrangement is done. Let the adhesive dry overnight.

Options and Extensions   This technique can also be used for candle rings, ornaments, and centerpieces. Any styrofoam form can be used with this technique. After the adhesive dries, decorate with ribbon, dried flowers, and so on.

The Dye Is Cast

Purpose   To use natural materials to make dye.

Description   After a discussion of the origins of dyeing techniques and purposes, students can participate in making natural dye baths for dyeing cloth or yarn.

Materials   Natural materials to be made into dye, water, boiling pots, sticks, campfire or hotplate, alum, cream of tartar, storage jars, white wool yarn.

Process   Collect natural materials. The following are some natural dyestuffs that may be used.

- Onion skins—light yellow

- Black walnut shells—dark brown

- Boysenberries or raspberries—pink and violet (berries need less water because of their moisture content)

- Blueberries—purple

- Raw beets—deep pink

- Sassafras root or bark—rose-brown

- Sunflower seeds—blue

- Madder—red

- Tea or coffee—light brown

- White iron-bark eucalyptus leaves, pods—orange

The amount of material needed for a dyepot varies; for four ounces of yarn, use 12 ounces of plant material, one ounce of alum, and 1/4 ounce of cream of tartar in four quarts of water.

Soak skeins of white wool and dyestuff in water for 24 hours. Simmer the dyestuff and wool for 15 minutes. Remove the wool from the pot. Stir in the alum and cream of tartar. Return the yarn to the pot.

Simmer everything for 30 minutes. Cool everything in pot overnight. Rinse yarn in cool water. Let the yarn dry. The dyebath can be used over again, although you might need to add more alum and cream of tartar to the pot.

Options and Extensions

This dye can easily be used for tie-dye projects or batik projects.

For tie-dyed cloth, use unbleached muslin or cotton (be sure the cloth is clean) and bind the cloth tightly using twine, rubber bands, or string. The material can be twisted, folded, or bundled up before binding. Immerse the cloth in hot dye until the desired color is obtained. Let the cloth dry and untie it. Press flat. Colors of the dyed cloth will not be so vivid as those of the dyed wool yarn.

For batik, use melted parafin to paint a design onto cotton cloth. Once the wax is cool, dye the cloth in a cold dye bath until the desired color is obtained. Let the cloth dry and iron it between layers of newsprint or brown paper bags to melt the wax out of the cloth.

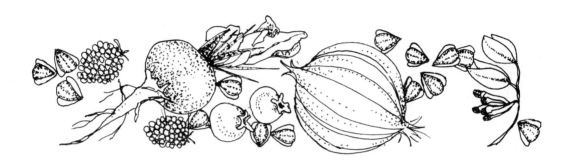

Weaving Adventure

Purpose

To provide a sequence of weaving experiences that will help develop motor skills, to gain an understanding of some concepts in weaving, and to increase awareness and understanding of basic spatial relationships (over/under, in/out, back/front, above/below).

Description

By actively using themselves as warp and/or weft, students should gain a feeling for weaving. This basic awareness can then be translated into projects in which students make their own looms and weave on them.

Materials

Objects in the school yard such as hurricane fences, jungle gyms, slides, ladders, railings; crepe paper streamers; long strips of cloth sewn together; rope; twine.

Process

Take the students to the playground. Have them form a large circle, hold hands, and spread out. Choose one student to go in and out of the circle, weaving between each child. Choose another student to hook up with the first one and continue weaving in and out. Keep choosing students to add onto the group weaving in and out.

Try weaving the line of students through something on the playground (swings, jungle gym).

Choose a school yard fence and let students weave their strips of crepe paper or cloth in and out, over and under. Discuss the warp and weft in weaving. What part does the fence play in weaving? What part did the students in the circle play?

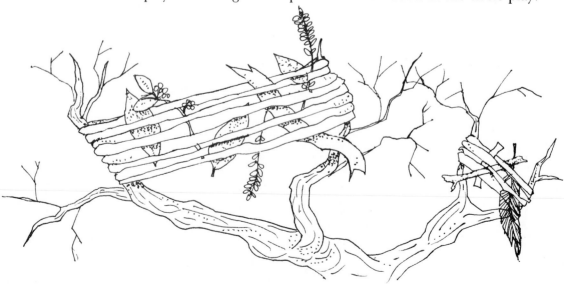

Chapter 4   Art Experiences in Nature

Options and Extensions

The students are now ready to make or find their looms. Have them look for things at home and discuss what they might use (shoe boxes, burlap, cheese cloth, mesh berry baskets, refrigerator or roasting racks, and so on).

Collect all sorts of fibers: string, yarn, reed, pipe cleaners, willow branches, dried weeds or grasses, and so on. (This is a good way to use the yarn students have dyed.) Let the students be creative with their weaving. Try to encourage the use of different colors and textures to improve the project's interest.

Free-form weaving can also be done on forked branches by wrapping the warp back and forth between the branches and then weaving into that warp. Objects such as shells, bark, boiled poultry bones, and feathers can also be incorporated into these woven projects.

Notes on the use of Art Experiences in Nature:

Explorations in Social Studies

"The world around him is the book in which without knowing it he is continually adding to the stores of memory, against the time when his judgment can profit by them."

Jean Jacques Rousseau

The American Indian, frontier life, mapping, natural resources, trade, and international relations are a few of the themes and units included in many social studies curricula. How might the out-of-doors be incorporated into these units and courses of study? What kinds of outdoor experiences will bring to life the gathering and processing of research information, and what outdoor experiences will make the concept of north, south, east, and west more concrete for elementary students?

These questions set the stage for the variety of activities included in this chapter. "Nature's Tools" and "Nature's Tool Box," for example, provide ideas for making Indian, pioneer, and primitive man units come to life on the school grounds. "Litter Analysis" and "Litter Lifelines" give students an opportunity to gather data and draw conclusions about their social environment. "School Yard Dig" focuses on archaeology and the excitement of processing finds.

The final series of outdoor activities in this chapter—including "Watch for North," "Compass Rose the School," and "Stepping Out"—deal with determining direction and learning map and compass skills.

Nature's Tools

Purpose   To explore specific environments, to collect natural objects, to describe the object's characteristics, and to identify its possible uses.

Description   Students collect natural objects in various outdoor settings— school yard, park, stream, beach, or woods. Students describe the objects' various features and identify possible tools these materials could make.

Materials   Paper, pencil, clipboard, plastic or paper collection bag.

Process   Help the class describe the various characteristics and qualities of a natural object. For example, a thistle is bristly, rigid, round, and spiny. Then identify uses for the thistle: paintbrush, decoration, curler, whisk. Talk with the class about why some natural objects might have been collected by people and how these objects could be used as tools. Have small teams of students hike through an area and collect various natural objects: pine cones, stones, grasses, reeds. Teams list the materials' characteristics and identify their possible uses. Then teams come together and share their findings.

Options and Extensions   Have students research Early American arts and crafts to determine what natural objects were used as tools.

Nature's Tool Box

Purpose
To identify specific features of simple tools and to locate natural objects that could be used or modified to make these tools.

Description
Students examine simple household tools, visit different outdoor environments—fields, streams, woods, ponds—locate natural objects, and shape these materials to make specific tools.

Materials
Clipboard, paper, pencil, plastic or paper collection bag.

Process
Pass out to individuals or small groups of students an assortment of simple tools: paper clips, sewing needle, letter opener, hair brush, straight pin, comb, and so on. Have students examine the tools carefully and decide what kinds of natural objects could be used or modified to make them. After students hike through an outdoor setting and collect materials, have them use the materials to make specific tools.

Options and Extensions
Assign all students the same tool and then let the class share their different approaches and finished products.

Litter Analysis

Purpose   To practice classifying material, interpreting data, and making inferences.

Description   Teams of students visit and collect litter at various outdoor facilities. They exchange findings, organize and classify the material to determine the setting in which the litter was found.

Materials   Plastic collection bag, clipboard, paper, pencil.

Process   Review classifying, drawing inferences, and interpreting data. For practice, provide students with an assortment of materials to classify and interpret. Divide class into several small groups and equip them with plastic trash bags. Have each group visit a different outdoor facility (playground, parking lot, athletic field, city park) and collect a complete sampling of litter. When the groups return, have them exchange bags. The students classify and interpret material in order to identify the kind of facility the litter came from and the people responsible for the litter (age, interest, tastes, activities). Have each group present its findings.

Options and Extensions   Discuss careers in which deductive reasoning skills are employed. Invite guests to come and discuss how data analysis is used in their work.

Social Studies

School Yard Dig

Purpose

To experience a simulation of an archaeological dig, to collect and classify data, and to interpret data findings.

Description

Students sift through piles of dirt or sand on the school yard and collect broken pieces of pottery or china. Students sort material, interpret findings, and piece objects back together.

Materials

Playground sandbox or piles of dirt and sand, collecting boxes, old china, wooden utensils, hammer, glue, screen, pencil, clipboard, shovel, garden gloves.

Process

Break an assorted collection of pottery and china and wooden utensils into different sized pieces and bury them in a sandbox or loose pile of dirt in the school yard. Review sorting and classification techniques used by archaeologists. Have students design data charts similar to the following:

Items Found	No. of Pieces	Material	Texture	Color	Markings
A	4	Glazed Pottery	Raised Design	Yellow & White	Flowered
B	5	Flower Pot Clay	Smooth	Red	None
C	4	Wood	Grained	Brown	Charred

Divide students into small teams and have each visit the dig site. After the groups collect and classify their materials, have each team share its finds and interpretations with the others. The groups then pool their findings and work together to reassemble the objects.

Options and Extensions

Invite an archaeologist to the school to share his or her work with the class or make arrangements to visit a real dig with an archaeologist.

Litter Lifelines

Purpose   To understand the relationship between natural resources and manufactured goods, to visualize the production process, to appreciate the value of recycling waste material, and to see the importance of using resources wisely.

Description   Students collect litter in an outdoor setting—school parking lot, playground, camp, or business district. Then each student selects a piece of trash—soda can, chewing gum wrapper, potato chip bag—and makes a life line of the litter, from the origin of its natural materials to its present state.

Materials   Shopping bag or box, paper, pencil, crayons, tape, string, paper-clips, 3 × 5 cards.

Social Studies

Process

Have the class discuss the relationship between natural resources and manufactured products, the contrast in time it takes to grow trees to maturity and the time it takes to produce paper, and the recycling of waste material. Pass out used shopping bags to students and hike through an outdoor area near the school—parking lot, playground, city park. After collecting a variety of litter, have each student select one item of trash and then graphically trace its lifeline from the origin of the litter's natural materials to its present condition.

For example, a gum wrapper might be traced to a tree cut and processed in Idaho, aluminum foil mined and manufactured in Alabama, oil for printers' ink pumped from deep beneath Texas' soil; all three natural resources were pooled in a package processing plant and then sent on their way to wrap the gum; the packaged gum was bought and consumed and the wrapper carelessly discarded behind home plate. Have students share and discuss their litter lifelines with the class.

Options and Extensions

Have each student write a creative story on the lifeline of his or her piece of litter. Research and imagination can be combined into an interesting story. Discuss recycling materials found on the litter hike. If possible make plans with the class to visit a recycling plant. Encourage students to identify ways the school might assist in recycling paper.

Shadow Shift

Purpose
To understand more concretely the earth's movement around the sun, to visualize the earth's rotation on its axis, and to observe the relationship between time of day and a shadow's length.

Description
Place a stick in the ground on a clear day and mark the length and position of its shadow. Return later to record the changes in the shadow's size and position—is it longer, shorter, or the same? Is it to the left or right of its former position?

Materials
Straight, pointed, two-foot stick, tape measure, yardstick, paper, pencil, clipboard.

Process
On a sunny day have students with partners place pointed sticks in the ground. Each team records the length and position of the stick's shadow. Ask the following questions: Will the shadow change its position? If so, will it be to the left or right of its original point? Will its length remain the same, or will it be longer or shorter? Answers need not be given. Have the class return in an hour to record the changes. Have students share their observations and relate their findings to the earth's rotation. Describe the relationship between time of day and the shadow's length.

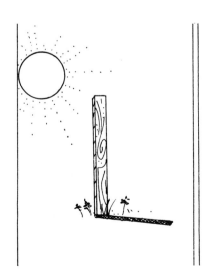

Options and Extensions
Select an object on the school grounds—flag pole, telephone pole—and record the change in the position of the object's shadow at a specific time of day each month of the school year.

Watch for North

Purpose

To determine direction without a compass.

Description

Students use a pocket or wrist watch and the shadow of a pencil placed adjacent to the watch to determine the approximate direction of north.

Materials

Pocket or wrist watch (nondigital), compass, pencil.

Process

Have students share ideas and information on how navigators determine direction without the use of a compass. Then on the playground have students place a pocket or wrist watch flat on the ground and hold a pencil upright near the edge of the watch. Turn the watch slowly until the hour hand is facing the sun and is in line with the pencil's shadow. Explain to the students that between 6:00 A.M. and 6:00 P.M. standard time, a line from the center of the watch dividing the *large* angle formed by the hour hand and 12:00 will point north. After the students have plotted north with their watches have them extend the line from the watch in the opposite direction to determine south. Verify their findings with a compass.

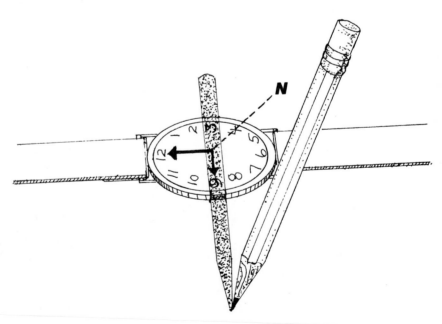

Options and Extensions

Have students research the history of the compass and encourage them to bring in any compasses they have.

Sun Watch

Purpose To locate north, to make the concept of directions more concrete, to illustrate the earth's rotation, and to visualize the earth's relation to the sun.

Description Students use a stick's shadow to determine directions.

Materials Pointed sticks approximately 3 feet in length, yardstick, compass.

Process Have students pair up. Give each team a pointed stick and a yardstick. On the school grounds have each group place the stick in the ground and carefully mark the tip of the stick's shadow. Have them return 20 minutes later and mark the tip of the stick's shadow a second time. Using a yardstick, have them form a line on the ground connecting the two marks. Ask the class why this line represents an east-west line. Discuss what needs to be done to determine the north-south line. Then have teams using the yardsticks draw a second line crossing the first at a right angle forming the north-south line. Verify the findings with a compass.

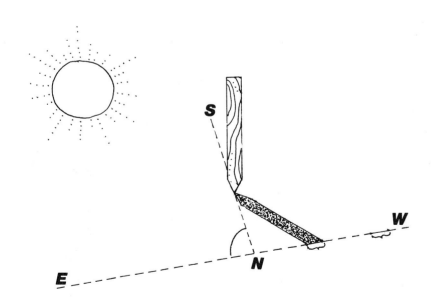

Options and Extensions Have the class research the history of the sundial. Have them make simple sundials, record their observations, and compare the dial's accuracy against a clock.

Compass Rose the School

Purpose
To visualize the positioning of the basic directions on a map, to develop skill in mapping, and to practice finding north.

Description
Students determine the direction of the school's main entrance, outline a map showing the top view of the school, and include a compass rose on the map.

Materials
Clipboard, pencil, paper, ruler, Silva® Orienteering® compass, pointed stick, yardstick, pocket or wrist watch.

Process
Review with the class the techniques used for determining direction without a compass. Divide students into small teams. Using the pocket watch or shadow tip method (see previous lessons in this chapter), have students determine which direction the school's main entrance is facing. Verify the findings with a compass. Have students then hike the perimeter of the building and sketch its outline, noticing the various exits. Have each team carefully outline a top view map of the school, including adjacent streets, and place a compass rose on it.

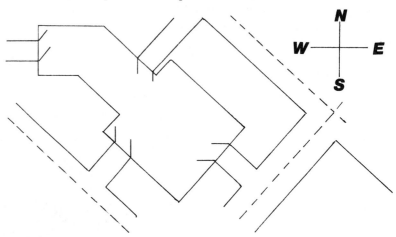

Options and Extensions
Have students make top view maps of their homes, determine directions, and adjacent streets, and include a compass rose.

Lost and Found

Purpose
To develop skill in using a compass and to practice following a bearing.

Description
Students learn the main parts of a compass and how to follow a specific bearing or direction. Working in pairs, students use each other as sighting points and leap-frog in a particular direction.

Materials
Compass (Silva Polaris® Type 7 Orienteering® compass is used in these activities).

Process
Introduce compasses by having students talk about what they would do if they were lost in the woods without one. Discuss what happens if a person tries to walk in a straight line out of a forest (one gradually moves in a circle). Explain why a compass is valuable (it determines direction and enables a person to move in a straight line through unfamiliar territory).

After this introducton, pass out Silva compasses and let students experiment with them as they hike to an open area near the school. While students share their observations about the compass, point out its three main parts: (1) plastic plate with direction-of-travel arrow, (2) red-tipped magnetic needle, and (3) compass housing with numbered degrees (see Figure A).

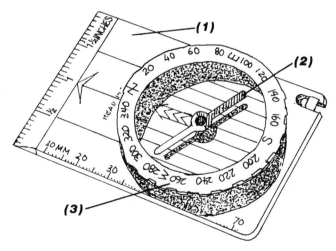

Figure A

Drawing courtesy of Silva® Compass, a division of Johnson Camping, Inc., Binghamton, New York.

To show the class how to follow a direction in a straight line, have them set the desired degree number (try 100 degrees) by turning the housing until the bearing (degree) is in line with the direction-of-travel arrow. Next, each student must orient the compass to the lay of the land. This is done by holding the compass in the palm, pointing the direction-of-travel arrow straight ahead (see Figure B), and turning the body until the red-tipped magnetic needle is *directly on top* of the arrow outlined in the housing (see Figure C). The direction-of-travel arrow is now pointing in the direction of 100 degrees.

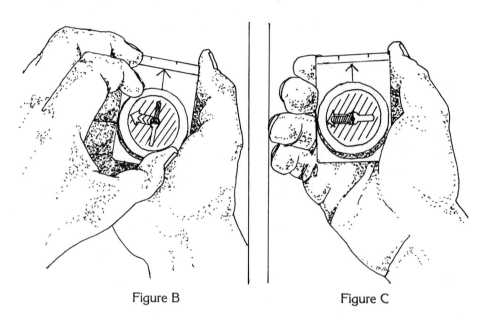

Figure B   Figure C

To follow the bearing of 100 degrees, have students pair up and set their compasses. The first team member sends his or her partner out in the approximate direction that the direction-of-travel arrow is pointing. The first team member tells the second to stop after about twenty yards (unless the field of vision is obscured). The first team member then lines the partner up with the direction-of-travel arrow by asking him or her to move to the left or right. Once this new position has been determined, the first team member moves ahead of the second and repeats the process. The partners leap-frog from one another down the field moving in the direction of 100 degrees.

A student working alone simply orients the compass to the lay of the land, identifies an object that is in line with the direction-of-travel arrow, moves to the other side of that object (the object substitutes for the partner in the original activity), and repeats the process.

Options and Extensions

Take the class to a wooded area and let them attempt to follow a bearing and move in a straight line. Have extra adults along to help.

Blaze a Trail

Purpose   To practice following a compass bearing and to develop skill in laying out a compass course.

Description   Teams of students (2 or 3 per group) set up compass courses with three different readings and check points. Each team exchanges its course with another group and follows the new one.

Materials   Pencil, note pad, Silva Polaris® Type 7 Orienteering® compass, paper plates, magic marker.

Process   Review how to follow a bearing; have students practice setting degree numbers and orienting the compass to the lay of the land. Before teams set up their courses, identify the following guidelines: all check points are marked by coded paper plates, degree readings are recorded on a course sheet, and a degree bearing is established or followed by standing *directly* on the plate.

Give each team four paper plates and a sheet of paper to record its degree readings. Team A (with its plates labeled A) places its starting point plate down and decides to go in the direction of 80°. After moving in that direction for 50 to 100 yards, a second plate is put down and a new direction (320°) is decided upon, sighted, and laid out. This process is repeated a third time with a degree reading of 165°, and after a certain distance, the final plate is placed. Team A's compass course sheet would read as follows:

Team A

Standing Pt.—80°
2nd Reading—320°
3rd Reading—165°

Instruct teams to partially cover their plates to make the courses more difficult for the other teams to follow. After the teams have laid out their courses, have them exchange sheets and follow the new course.

Options and Extensions   Set up the Silva® School Yard Compass Game on the blacktop. Order from: Orienteering® Services, USA
        Box 1604 Binghamton, New York 13902-0966

Social Studies

Compass Square-Off

Purpose
To practice following a bearing, to develop skill in pacing, to make geometric shapes more concrete.

Description
On the playground students plot squares using a compass to determine the four right angles forming the square.

Materials
Silva Polaris® Type 7 Orienteering® compass, paper plates, pencil, paper.

Process
Review the steps for following a bearing (Lost and Found activity in this chapter); give students an opportunity to practice this skill on the playground. Identify with the class a square's characteristics and introduce the following steps for making a square on the playground: Select a degree direction and follow it for certain number of paces, add 90° to the first degree direction and follow it for the same number of paces. Repeat this process two more times, adding 90° for each new bearing (see example below).

Have students pair up for this project and provide each team with a set of paper plates to mark the corners of the square. Have the class identify and discuss any problem they had completing the assignment.

Options and Extensions
Students could try making other geometric shapes, such as rectangles, equilateral triangles, and so on. For an equilateral triangle students would add 120° to determine each new degree direction.

Out of Sight

Purpose
To learn the technique of finding a direction, and to practice following a degree bearing.

Description
The technique is learned for finding a direction with a compass and a situation is identified for using it.

Materials
Silva Polaris® Type 7 Orienteering® compass, paper plates, paper, pencil.

Process
Have the class review and then practice the steps used to follow a direction with a compass: (1) line up degree number with the direction-of-travel arrow, (2) point the direction-of-travel arrow ahead of you, (3) turn slowly until the red-tipped magnetic needle is directly on top of the fancy arrow inside the housing, (4) then move along the path that the direction-of-travel arrow is pointing.

Discuss a situation in which the technique of finding a direction is used. For example, you are standing on one side of a ravine and sighting a tree that you would like to observe closely but would have difficulty finding after crossing the ravine. Have students practice finding a direction using the following steps (see figures A and B below): (1) point direction-of-travel arrow to desired landmark; (2) turn compass housing until the red-tipped magnetic needle is directly on top of the fancy arrow inside the housing; (3) read the bearing opposite the direction-of-travel arrow on housing; and (4) follow the bearing.

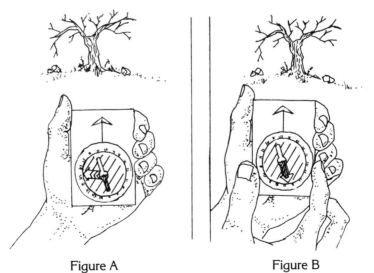

Figure A   Figure B

Social Studies

On the schoolgrounds let students practice finding the degree direction of different objects, such as a tree, the flag pole, and other school landmarks. To assess the student's ability to find a direction, set up a course in which the students have to stand on certain spots (marked with numbered paper plates) and find the bearings of predetermined landmarks. The score sheet for such a course could be as follows:

Pt. 1   Direction to flagpole _____
degree reading

Pt. 2   Direction to pine tree _____
degree reading

Pt. 3   Direction to school's chimney _____
degree reading

Options and Extensions

Visit a ravine and have students use the compass to find a bearing of a landmark on the other side. Students then follow this bearing across the ravine to the object.

Looking Back

Purpose

To learn to return from a degree bearing and to practice following a direction.

Description

After following a degree direction, students learn how to reverse a bearing without resetting the compass in order to return to a starting point.

Materials

Silva Polaris® Type 7 Orienteering® compass.

Process

Identify situations in which a person would need to reverse a degree bearing and backtrack to a starting point. For example, you have left valuables behind or lost something en route. Explain that reversing a direction 180° is done by pointing the direction-of-travel arrow toward you, orienting the compass to the lay of the land, and walking against the direction-of-travel arrow.

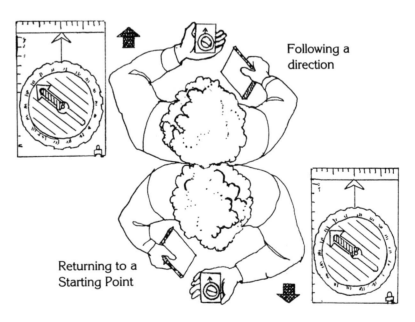

Following a direction

Returning to a Starting Point

On the playground have students practice following a direction for several hundred feet and then return from it to the starting point. Partially cover starting points to offer students a greater challenge when returning from a bearing.

Options and Extensions

Visit a forested area and have students follow and return from a certain bearing.

Stepping Out

Purpose
To practice the technique of following compass bearings for specified distances.

Description
Teams of students (2 or 3 per group) begin at a central point and move through a compass course following a series of bearings for specific distances.

Materials
Silva Polaris® Type 7 Orienteering® compass, clipboard, pencil, course cards.

Process
Before beginning the activity, have students practice pacing for accuracy and review steps for following a bearing.

Each team is given a course card—see sample below—listing the bearings and the distances in feet for each reading.

```
                    Course Card

          Starting Point: Flagpole

              Go 45 degrees for 100 ft.

              Then go 258 degrees for 65 ft.

              Then go 120 degrees for 130 ft.

              Then go 0 degrees for 40 ft.
```

At five-minute intervals, the teams begin the course and proceed through the different bearings. Each part of the course should lead to a certain object or point: tree, bush, flagpole, corner of building (see illustration).

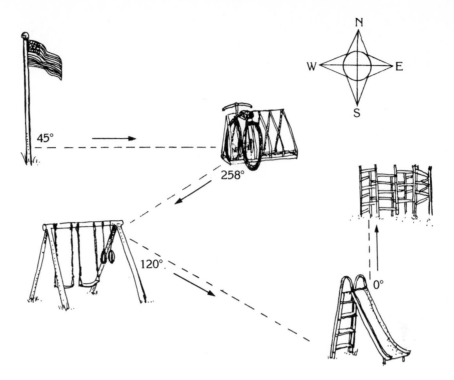

Once a team has completed the course the students identify the final object. If they are wrong, encourage them to try it again.

Options and Extensions

Set up the Silva® Compass competition game in the school yard. Order from Orienteering® Services, USA, Box 1604, Binghamton, New York, 13902-0966.

Notes on the use of Social Studies Explorations:

Science Beyond the Classroom

"The lasting pleasures of contact with the natural world are not reserved for scientists but are available to anyone who will place himself under the influence of earth, sea, and sky and their amazing life."

Rachel Carson

Science in the out-of-doors begins with developing sense perceptions rather than with developing an organized body of knowledge in some logical manner, as it is presented in the classroom. The things we see, smell, handle, hear, and taste are then presented in a total science context.

The student recognizes the features of the natural world and becomes aware of the relationships of all living and nonliving things: air, water, soil, sunlight, animals, and plants. The study of these relationships through changing seasons and weather conditions provides opportunities for students to learn both elementary science concepts and the most complex aspects of ecology.

This chapter leads students to discoveries within a shovelful of soil in "Exploring for Earthlings" and examines the interface of the natural to the man-made world in "Asphalt Jungle," "Wildflower Hunt," and "Adopt a Tree." The study of plant life in a holistic and personal sense is encouraged. In every case, the activities are designed to provide direct experiences in science while developing a feeling of familiarity toward the out-of-doors and enriching the knowledge gained through the classroom and textbook.

Exploring for Earthlings

Purpose To realize that a small piece of ground can support a myriad of animal life, to help establish methods of recording observable data.

Description Students work in small groups to remove a cubic foot of soil from the ground and analyze it. They record all findings of animal life, compare samples with other groups, and return the soil to its original position.

Materials Small shovel or spade; large piece of white paper; sticks, spoons, tweezers, and other objects for digging and poking; ruler; magnifying glass; data sheet; clipboard; pencil.

Process Take students to a location where they can dig holes without destroying someone's lawn or an athletic field. Have small groups of four or five students dig up a cubic foot of soil and place it on the white paper. Have them slowly poke and pick away at the soil, carefully studying it with a magnifying glass. As the groups find animals, they should record their findings on a data sheet similar to the one shown below.

Group _____ Name _____			
Location of Soil Sample:			
Appearance of Soil:			
What did you find?			
Name (if unknown, assign a number)	Description	How many?	Sketch
1.			
2.			
3.			

The group should compare their findings by visiting each site and noting the specimens. Discussion can center on kinds of animal life and their abundance; animal classification (insect, spider, worm); differences in soil composition; relationships of soil type and specimens.

When study of a site is completed, all the soil should be restored to the spot.

Options and Extensions

Make a bucket microscope for each group (or have the group make it themselves). Cut several holes in the sides near the bottom of a cardboard bucket or tub. Make the holes big enough so that students can put their hand in. Then put a large piece of plastic wrap over the top of the bucket and secure it by stretching a rubber band tightly around it. Pour water slowly into the plastic so it begins to stretch and sag down into the bucket. Place an insect in the bottom of the bucket. Look through the water to see a magnified insect. Add more water to make the specimen appear bigger.

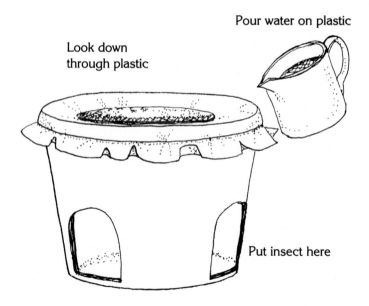

Pour water on plastic

Look down through plastic

Put insect here

Getting Degrees

Purpose

To develop and practice skills in reading a thermometer, to recognize outdoor temperature variance during the day, to demonstrate temperature differences by use of a bar graph, to become familiar with both Fahrenheit and Celsius thermometer readings.

Description

Students take temperature readings (both Celsius and Fahrenheit, if desired) at different times of the day in different locations on the school grounds. They compare and contrast the readings and give reasons for the changes in temperature. Student data is recorded on a bar graph.

Materials

Outdoor thermometers, a tube and foil to make a shield in which to place each thermometer, colored pencils or crayons, pencil, paper, time piece, worksheet for the bar graph or commercial graph paper.

Process

Demonstrate how to read a thermometer correctly. Divide the class into groups of three or four.

Take the groups outdoors. Have each group select and carefully mark a spot away from brick walls. Then have the groups take temperature readings at 9:30 A.M., 11:00 A.M., 12:30 P.M., and 2:00 P.M.

When recording the temperature, have one student hold the thermometer in a shield one meter from the ground for a two-minute period. Have another student read the temperature at the end of the two-minute period. Have a third student record the reading. The next time the group takes a reading, have different members of the groups hold the thermometer, take the reading, and write down the temperature so that everyone gets a chance to read the thermometer.

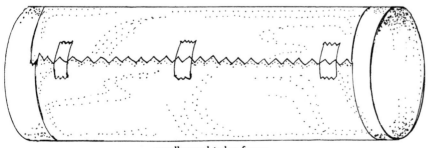

aluminum foil wrapped around exterior of cardboard tube

cardboard tube from paper towel roll

Have each group share its findings by making a bar graph to show the temperatures in the various spots at the different times of the day. Use a worksheet that has been marked in degrees along the vertical and hours along the horizontal.

Tape each group's worksheet on the wall or board for each of the sample times and have the students compare and discuss their findings.

Options and Extensions

Give students different places to determine the temperature. For example:

	Temperature	
	°F	°C
In your hand		
On the ground		
On a stone		
Under some leaves		
In the shade		
In the light		
Your own place		

Most daily newspapers carry a list of the day's temperature highs and lows across the nation. Have students record temperature readings at major cities on an outline map of the United States. Note the day's high and low for a selected number of cities. Keep records of these for several weeks, graph the results, and compare the differences.

Now You See It, Now You Don't

Purpose
To stimulate visual awareness, to introduce the concept of protective coloration and natural camouflage.

Description
Students look for colored strips of paper in a grassy area. Natural camouflage or coloration prevents some colors from being found easily. Data are collected and results are interpreted.

Materials
Blank chart; 40 feet of string; 4 stakes; 100 strips of colored paper, 1″ × 1/4″ (red, yellow, green, and blue—25 of each).

Process
Make a 10 ft. square in the grass with the string and stakes. Scatter the colored strips randomly within the square. Do not let the students look while you do this. Give five or six students at a time 60 seconds to find as many strips as possible. Record the results of each group on the chart shown below. Then compare and discuss the results.

GROUP	Red	Yellow	Green	Blue
1				
2				
3				
4				
5				
6				

The brighter colors will be easier to see in the grass.

Options and Extensions
Have students observe plants or animals on the school grounds or near their homes. Ask them how these animals and plants are protected by natural camouflage. This can lead to a discussion, library project, or activity about other ways in which animals and plants protect themselves from their enemies.

As the Twig Twirls

Purpose　　　To experience the problems of proper balance and the principle of the lever, to make an art-science display using natural materials.

Description　　Students make mobiles using twigs, small branches, and other natural materials.

Materials　　Strong twigs (those with branches make it more exciting), thread, tape, pine cones or other natural objects, twine, glue.

Process　　Have students collect twigs or branches of various sizes and other natural objects such as pine cones, acorns, leaves, berries, and so on.

　　Students need adequate working space to suspend the objects while constructing the mobiles. Tightly string several strands of heavy twine across the room.

　　Have students tie one end of a long piece of thread to one of the twigs. (It does not matter where it is tied; it can be moved later.) Have them tie the other end of the thread to the twine running across the room. Make sure the twig hangs well above the floor. Have students cut several pieces of thread and tie one piece to one of the objects they collected. Tie the object to one end of the twig, using a loose knot. The object will make the twig tilt to one side. Have them take another twig, tie a piece of thread to it, and attach it to the first twig. Slide the object and second twig until they are balanced.

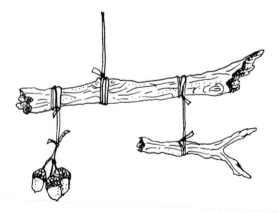

Have students hang two objects from the second twig. Slide the objects back and forth until they balance.

Tighten all the knots, put a dab of glue or tape on each one, and hang the mobile. Allow time for students to discuss the concepts involved in balancing and working levers (fulcrum, effort arm, and so on).

Note: For older students, many more branches can be added for more creativity and a greater challenge. As the students work on their mobiles, they will experience the problems of obtaining proper balance and of preventing objects from touching. For solutions, they will need to think about variables such as object size and shape, thread length, best positions for objects, and best fastening place.

Options and Extensions

Themes can be developed for mobiles. For example, if birds, mammals, vertebrates, or leaves represent the main theme, appropriate objects or pictures can be used as the balancing pieces.

Science Seeker

Purpose

To increase awareness of the out-of-doors and its many natural science phenomena, to increase student knowledge of individual science concepts.

Description

Working in pairs, students are given a list of items to find on a science scavenger hunt. They either bring back the found objects or a description of their location and setting. Explanations of the findings are shared back in the classroom.

Materials

Plastic bag, notebook, pencil, and paper, small plastic container (approximately 1/2 pint) or baby food jar.

Process

Give students a list of items to find on or near the school grounds (adapt the list for a city park or camp environment). Devise a point distribution based on the degree of difficulty in finding the objects if additional competition is desired. Group students in pairs and set a specific time limit depending on the nature of the items in the hunt and the geographic area.

The science scavenger hunt teaches science as well as an awareness of the out-of-doors. Carefully select the items and explain what they are or have the students research each one before or after the activity. It is important for you to make sure enough of the items or examples can be found in the area where the hunt is taking place.

When the students return, have them show the objects they found and share explanations of these items in terms of description, location, interpretation, and unusual findings. Encourage students to take notes during the scavenger hunt to help with the sharing session.

Two lists that can be used for a scavenger hunt are outlined on page 113. Be sure to remind students not to pick or uproot any living plants.

Universal List

1. Some animal trace
2. A producer, a consumer, a decomposer
3. A stick that looks like an animal
4. Three different wild flowers
5. A manufactured object that is weathered
6. Objects representing the primary colors
7. A live animal to fit in plastic container or baby food jar
8. A spider web
9. Three simple geometric shapes in nature
10. An object with a pleasant smell

Special Environment

1. Insect gall
2. Water strider
3. Shell fungus
4. Jewel weed
5. Acorn or acorn cap
6. A piece of shale
7. Moss
8. Pine cone
9. Maple leaf
10. Seed pod

Options and Extensions

Items students are to find on the scavenger hunt can be put in the form of clues and catchy two liners. For example:

"You're going strong now! Add *1 yellowish leaf.*
Next break off *4 thorns* but don't cause any grief."

"Locate a honeysuckle bush for some fun.
A *berry* from it is item number one."

Students can help in this process by making up science scavenger hunts and exchanging the approved lists.

Science

Six Legs Are Faster Than Two

Purpose
To determine the variable speed derived by measuring distance and time, to practice observation and measurement skills, to record data, to make interpretations about sampling techniques.

Description
Students determine how fast ants can move per second or minute. They determine average speed by observing distance and time.

Materials
Sheets of newsprint, paper cup, pencil, ruler, a piece of thread or string, a time piece.

Process
Students choose partners and go outside to look for a supply of ants. Have the students find several ants and put them into a small paper cup. If more than one type of ant can be found in your area, have students collect data on several species.

Have students place a sheet on the ground. One student puts an ant near the center of the sheet while the other student tracks it with a pencil. There will be some error because students will not be able to track the ant exactly. The student who put the ant on the paper should keep a record of the amount of time it takes the ant to go off the paper. Then have students take a piece of thread and lay it out along part of the track, pick it up, straighten it out, and measure it with a ruler. They should continue until they have measured the entire length of the track. Students repeat the procedure using different ants of the same species and compute their average speed.

I. Brown Ant	Time (sec.)	Distance (cm or inches)	Speed (cm/sec. or inches/sec.)
Ant #1			
Ant #2			
Ant #3			
Average			

II. Black Ant	Time (sec.)	Distance (cm or inches)	Speed (cm/sec. or inches/sec.)
Ant #1			
Ant #2			
Ant #3			
Average			

Return to the classroom, compare data, and discuss the findings. The following questions will help guide the discussion:

1. What length of time is best for accurate readings of the data?

2. Can you assume that all ants travel at the same speed? How would you set up an investigation to determine this? How many ants would be necessary to determine the speed of a certain species?

3. How reliable are your measurements of the track? If you repeat the measurements of the track, how closely do they agree?

4. Are there better ways of tracking the ants and getting more accurate measurements?

Options and Extensions

Combine each pair's average track length and graph the distance covered per minute by the entire sample of ants. Determine the class average, remember that the larger the sample, the more accurate the information that has been collected.

Science

Energy Run

Purpose

To become acquainted with the idea of a food chain and aware of the relationship between producer, consumer, predator, and prey; to illustrate the dependence of all animals and plants on their environment.

Description

Students simulate members of a food chain, either animals or plants (including human beings). They play a game of tag in which they try to avoid being caught while they obtain enough energy to stay in the game. At the end of a specified period of time the game is stopped and the class looks to see where the energy has accumulated and which animals or plants have survived.

Materials

Construction paper, scissors, marking pens, and string to make signs; stakes, flags, or masking tape for marking boundaries outside the school; about 10 times as many pieces of candy, peanuts, or cardboard markers as students participating; a container marked "Used Up Energy."

Process

Choose an area about 50 ft. × 50 ft. with clearly marked boundaries (a school yard or part of an athletic field will do with the boundaries marked using stakes or flags). Have students pick role assignments out of a hat and make their own signs, using construction paper and string. Each kind of animal or plant has a different colored sign with the animal or plant's name printed on it in large letters. About 1/3 of the students should be plants, 1/3 plant eaters, and 1/3 animal eaters. One student plays the sun. You may want to research and discuss different food chains with the class.

Designate places of protection (or homes) for the animals, for example, an owl by a tree, a skunk by a fence, or a grasshopper by a bush. One person is identified as the sun and has energy in the form of candy, peanuts, or cardboard markers.

Rules for the game

1. This is a game of tag.

2. The person who is the sun stands in one place.

3. At the beginning of the game, the only person who has any energy is the sun.

4. The sun gives energy to the plants in units of four to start the game. When the plants run out of energy, they go to the sun and get more.

5. All the animals start at their home, which is safe. They leave home and hunt for lunch. Those animals that do not hunt or cannot catch food are considered dead of starvation at the end of the game.

6. The plants run away from the animals who are trying to catch them.

7. The animals can only get energy if they can catch and tag a plant or animal (that they can eat). Two units are given up at each tag and one of the two goes into a container marked "Used Up Energy."

8. Animals can get energy from plants or other animals as often as they can catch them.

At a signal start the game and watch the interaction. When the activity starts to run down, stop the game (this will vary with age groups). Gather everyone together and see where the energy has accumulated. Discuss the following questions:

A. Where does all energy come from? How is some of it used up? How do animals get more energy?

B. What animal is at the top of the food chain? What is at the bottom?

C. What would happen if all the owls were gone? What if all the mice were gone?

D. Can an animal be both predator and prey? Give examples.

E. Will you need more grasshoppers or more owls for a good food chain?

F. What are producers? What are consumers?

Options and Extensions

Assign students different roles as parts of the environment (sun, air, water, and soil). Connect them with one continuous strand of string and explain their relationship to one another (students could research their roles at this point). Cut the string and discuss what happens if this web of life is interrupted.

Asphalt Jungle

Purpose   To observe the intersect between one part of the man-made world and the natural environment and to study the cause and effect relationships between them, to practice collecting and interpreting results from a science investigation.

Description   Student groups study an asphalt area and find effects of its interaction with man and the natural environment. Evidence is gathered through guided observation of some specific differences, and the results are interpreted.

Materials   Markers (coat hangers or string), ruler, string, data sheet, pencil.

Process   Provide students with a one square foot marker (a coat hanger bent into a square or a piece of string). Take the class to different areas around the school and neighborhood where they can find asphalt paving. Students working individually or in pairs lay out their markers in different locations on this jungle safari and collect the following data:

1. Number of cracks
2. Width of the widest crack
3. Length of the longest crack (use a string laid out along the crack and then measure it)
4. Roughness of surface (help students make a simple 1-3 scale based on some sample pieces of asphalt)
5. Description of color
6. Number of plants
7. Height of the tallest plant

Students should record their findings on a data sheet, as shown below, and then compare results.

Asphalt Jungle Investigation

	Sample I	Sample II	Sample III	Sample IV
Number of cracks				
Width of widest crack				
Length of longest crack				
Roughness of surface				
Color				
Number of plants				
Height of tallest plant				

Discussion of the results might include some of the following questions:

A. What effects do plants have on asphalt? (Consider roots and chemicals in this question.)

B. Which area had the most cracks and the widest cracks? What might have caused this?

C. What might be the cause of the difference in roughness of the surface?

D. Were there color differences between sample areas? What might have caused this?

E. Would freezing water have an effect on asphalt paving?

Options and Extensions

Play the "Growing Plant Game." Divide the students into groups and assign each group an area of the asphalt. They are to look for plant life in the cracks. Assign 1 point for a square inch section of grass, 2 points for each leafy plant, and 3 points for each flowery plant.

Science

Stop, Look, and Leaf

Purpose

To develop skills of observation and description, to determine useful characteristics in describing and identifying leaves, to acquaint students with some standard botanical nomenclature.

Description

Working in small groups, students simulate scientific expeditions to other planets to collect samples of plant life. They concentrate on leaf types, find samples, and describe leaves using botanical vocabulary and their own words.

Materials

Notebook or clipboard, paper, pencil.

Process

Role-play with the class scientists from outer space looking for planets with an environment that will support the kind of vegetation found on earth. Explain to them that they will be divided into four groups and that each task force is to collect samples of 6–8 different kinds of leaves. Have each task force take notes on the surrounding environment for the samples they collect, taking care to record specific information. Tell the groups to work independently, assign them an area of outer space, and give them a time limit.

After returning to the classroom, have each task force write up descriptions of their samples. Separate the four groups physically so they cannot see or hear each other while they write descriptions of each leaf sample.

The importance of accurate descriptions should be emphasized; mention the following two rules: (1) all descriptions must be written (*no drawings*); and (2) correct plant names cannot be used even if they are known.

To ensure that students work successfully with these ideas, discuss ways of describing leaves. The following list of definitions is a suggested guide to begin your discussion with the class:

Type of leaf

- *Simple leaf*—one blade or leaflet per leaf

- *Compound leaf*—two or more leaflets per leaf

- *Pinnately compound*—leaflets on each side of a central shaft

- *Palmately compound*—leaflets radiate from a central point

Venation (vein pattern)

- *Pinnate venation*—all main leaf veins arise from the central shaft or midrib

- *Palmate venation*—three or more veins radiate from a central point

Base of leaf

- *Assymmetrical*—base of leaf blade is not the same on each side of midrib

- *Symmetrical*—base of leaf blade is the same on each side of midrib

- *Wedge-shaped*—base of leaf appears triangular or leveled

Leaf arrangement

- *Opposite*—leaves arise opposite each other on stem

- *Alternate*—leaves arise alternately from each other on stem

- *Whorled*—several leaves arise from nearly the same point on a stem

Options and Extensions

The task force may wish to make a master of corrected descriptions of samples to be sent back to earth (this could be put on a bulletin board or given to another class for their own excursion).

Tree and shrub guides can be used to illustrate botanical nomenclature and scientifically name the plants.

Pair up students and have one describe a leaf using their newly acquired language. Have other student draw the leaf. Partners switch roles and repeat the process using a different leaf.

Adopt a Tree

Purpose
To learn about the structure, function, and life cycle of a tree as an example of the plant kingdom; to help students become aware of the interrelationships of the tree and its environment.

Description
A student observes and keeps records on one tree from September through May. The study of a single tree permits close observation, familiarity through the five senses, and the personalization of a vast array of knowledge.

Materials
Paper, pencil, notebook.

Process
In September, ask each student to choose a tree that is located where it can be observed frequently. A tree on the school grounds or near the student's home is recommended; one in his or her yard or a neighbor's yard is probably the easiest to work with. Students keep their tree records in notebooks. The cover of the notebook can be decorated as an art lesson ("Sun Silhouettes" or "Rub It Out" in Chapter 4, Art Experiences in Nature would be excellent projects for this purpose).

The following questions and directions are suggested for the first step:

1. What type of tree did you select?
2. Why did you select this particular tree?
3. Exactly where is this tree located?
4. Give your tree a name.
5. Describe your tree right now.
   A. Height (Estimate using your height or the height of a house, garage, or some other object.)
   B. Distance around (use hands, arms, belt, or string to estimate.)
   C. Leaves (type, size, structure, color)
   D. Fruit (type, size, color)
   E. Bark (color, texture, design)
   F. Any other interesting characteristics
6. Draw sketches of your tree from several angles, including the position of the leaves on the branches and the position of the branches on the tree.

We suggest beginning the observation in the fall. Have students begin collecting data on their tree.

1. Record the following observations about their tree every other week:

    Note the date.

    Estimate the number of leaves (more suitable for saplings).

    Color and sketch the leaves (or take snapshots).

    In conjunction with collecting this data, present a lesson in estimation. Discuss the following points:

    What is an estimate?
    Where and how can estimates be used?
    How can estimating be used to count the number of leaves on a tree?

    One technique is to count the number of leaves on a branch or two as close to the ground as possible and then to count the number of branches and multiply.

2. Complete a series of measurement activities:

    Calculate the circumference and diameter of your tree. Estimate its height using the shadow ratio and isosceles right triangle methods (these activities can be found in the math chapter).

3. Observe and record the following data.

    What was the approximate date when the autumn colors first appeared in the leaves?

    What were the principal color changes? What were the other colors?

    What was the first date leaves began falling from the tree?

    Most of the leaves fell in what two-week period?

    When did the very last leaves fall from the crown?

    Without leaves, how are the twigs arranged on the branches?

4. What animals are using the tree for food, shelter, or housing? This information can be used for classroom discussion with students adding their individual observations.

Winter tree observations can include the following questions and activities for the students:

1. What do you notice first when you look at your tree in the winter? What changes occurred?
2. Sketch and describe your tree on a sunny day; on a moonlit night; in the snow; in the rain.
3. Describe the bark. Make a bark rubbing.
4. When it snows, how does your tree look? Observe and record tracks and other signs of animal life in or near your tree; the base of the tree right after a snowfall and two days later; the position of snow on trunk and limbs.
5. Sketch the tree's shadow in an art medium you like.

Spring observation can include the following questions:

1. When did new leaves appear from the buds on the tree?
2. When did the first blossoms appear on the tree? When did the last blossoms disappear?
3. When did the tree first have well-formed fruit on it?

Options and Extensions

Trees offer a great variety of special topics that can be developed. Two units are suggested and outlined here as examples:

Trees and their products:

1. Research important uses of lumber.
2. Research the manufacture of furniture and the types of lumber used in this industry.
3. Research veneer and its uses.
4. Research uses of wood pulp.
5. Research the uses of sugars that make up wood fibers.

Do a statistical analysis of trees. Include the following in a sample set of 25 trees:

1. Compare types of trees and shapes of trees (30 yards from base).
2. Compare smooth-barked trees and rough-barked trees and whether they are scented or odorless.
3. Compare tree heights (shadow-ratio method).
4. Compare circumference and diameter of the trees.
5. Compare frequency distributions using numbers 1, 2, 3, and 4.
6. Find mode, median, mean, and range using the frequency distributions.
7. Compute percents for data collected (example: 10 percent oak trees).
8. Organize data from numbers 1, 2, 3, and 4 and present it in a vertical bar graph.

Wildflower Hunt: Bring Them Back Alive

Purpose   To observe wildflowers, to identify the main parts, to develop an appreciation for their abundance and variety.

Description   Take the class on a wildflower hunt around their school or neighborhood. Each student chooses one wildflower to bring back and study. (Discretion should be used when picking wildflowers, both in terms of number and kind. Caution students to pick only one and to choose a location in which there are a number of common varieties.)

Materials   Paper, pencil, crayons and other drawing materials.

Process   Wildflowers grow almost everywhere. They can be found in fields, backyards, curblawns, roadsides, and city lots. Different weeks of the year will find different flowers in bloom. Lead the class on a hike around the school and neighborhood, looking for "weeds" in your area, and have each student pick one wildflower (it is not essential that each student have a different kind of flower as there probably will not be enough varieties in your limited area). After choosing a wildflower, have each student find out more about it by looking at specific details, as are shown in the drawings on the following pages. Have each student fill out an information sheet on his or her flower, completing these sentences:

My wildflower has _____ . (kind of flower head)

My wildflower's petals are _____ .

My wildflower has _____ . (kind of corolla)

My wildflower's leaves are _____ .

My wildflower's leaf arrangement is _____ .

My wildflower's leaf margin is _____ .

Science

PARTS OF A FLOWER

PETALS

Petals Separate

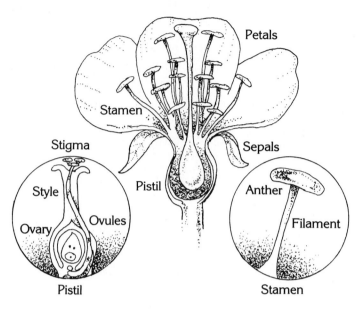

Petals Joined
(individual
lobes cannot
be removed)

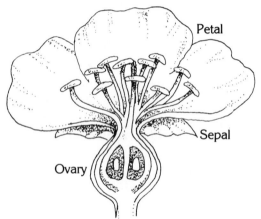

**Composite
Flower Head**

The composite family is the largest family of flowering plants in North America and the second largest in the world. Each flower in a composite is actually made up of many flowers grouped together as a *flower head*. Two kinds of flowers can be seen in the composite family:

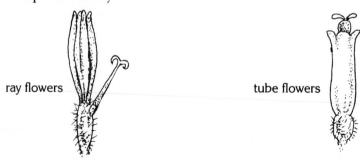

With these two kinds of flowers, three types of flower heads are possible:

Many Tube Flowers
Surrounded by Ray Flowers
(New England Aster)

Many Ray Flowers
(Sow Thistle)

Many Tube Flowers
(Bull Thistle)

VARIATIONS IN PETALS

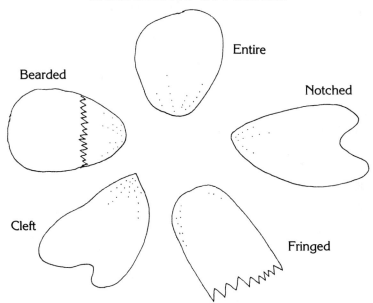

Entire

Bearded

Notched

Cleft

Fringed

TYPE OF COROLLA

Simple Shaped

3 petals
4 petals
5 petals
6 petals

Elongated Clusters

(elongated masses of flowers
tightly or somewhat loosely
arranged along the stalk)

Daisy and Dandelion Shaped

(many radiating petals—ray flowers)

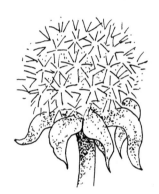

Rounded Clusters

(rounded masses of flowers either
tightly or loosely arranged on a stalk)

Odd Shaped

(unusual overall appearance—bilaterally symmetrical)

LEAVES

Simple　　　　　　Compound

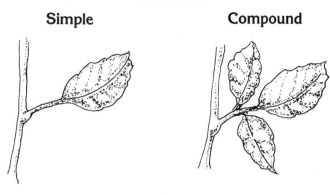

ARRANGEMENT OF LEAVES

Basal
(close to the
ground)

Alternate

Whorled

Opposite

LEAF MARGINS

Entire　　　　　　**Toothed**

Undulate　　**Lobed**　　**Spiked**

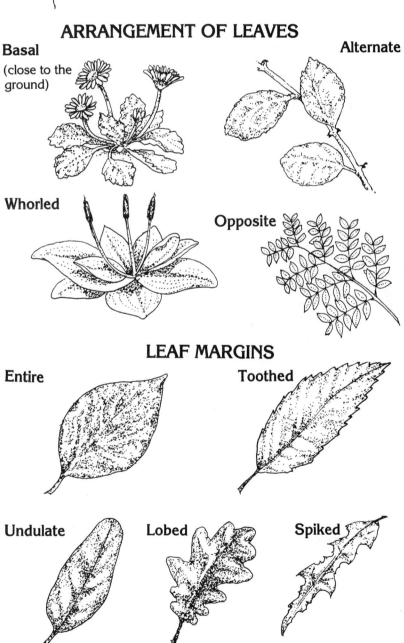

Science

Have students note the different characteristics along with other observations about their flower (odor, location, color, height, and date in bloom. Have the students draw and color their wildflower, labeling some or all of the specific characteristics described. Naming and personalizing their wildflower makes it particularly special; fictious and imaginary names should be encouraged, although identification and finding the real name may also be an objective. Students should share their wildflowers and findings with the rest of the class.

Options and Extensions

Have students write an essay or build a story around their wildflowers or make a mobile with the colored wildflower pictures.

Some suggested reference books

Dana, Mrs. William Starr. *How to Know the Wildflowers*. New York: Dover Publications, Inc., 1963.

Newcomb, Lawrence. *Newcomb's Wildflower Guide*. Boston—Toronto: Little, Brown and Company, 1977.

Peterson, Roger Tory and Margaret McKenny. *A Field Guide to Wildflowers of Northeastern and North-Central North America*. Boston: Houghton Mifflin Company, 1968.

Zim, Herbert S. and Alexander C. Martin. *Flowers: A Guide to Familiar American Wildflowers*. Racine, Wis.: Western Publishing Company, Inc., 1950.

Weather or Not?

Purpose
To use the naturally changing conditions of the environment and selected locations to do a scientific study including data collection, analysis, and interpretation of results.

Description
Students make simple weather instruments to determine wind direction and speed. Weather information is recorded at different locations around the school using these instruments. The results are tabulated, analyzed, and interpreted.

Materials
Pencils, weather study chart, yardstick or meter stick, anemometer, nephoscope, wind vane, compass, thermometer.

Process
Explain and demonstrate the use of the anemometer, wind vane, thermometer, nephoscope, and compass. Divide the class into groups of 4 or 5 students and give each group a weather study chart. Explain the plan for collecting data and discuss possible sites on the school grounds for accomplishing this task. Emphasize the importance of finding a variety of interesting stations for data collection: open field, parking lot (blacktop area), north side of the building.

Students should be given a time limit depending on their age group and the geographic locations selected. When students return to the classroom, allow time for each group to discuss results and prepare a summary of their findings. Bring the small groups together and have each make a report and compare the results of their scientific study.

Science

WEATHER STUDY CHART

Nephoscope Reading

(Beginning of Study) _____   (End of Study) _____

Readings	Station A	Station B	Station C	Station D	Station E
Wind Direction					
Wind Speed at Ground Level					
Wind Speed at 1 m or 1 yd.					
Temperature at Ground Level					
Temperature at 1 m or 1 yd.					
General Description of Station Environments					

Temperature Readings: Check thermometers in a controlled environment first; keep thermometers outside; be careful how you hold thermometers; allow one minute for thermometers to adjust to a new location.

Wind Speed: Speeds should be reported in revolutions per minute.

MAKING THE WEATHER INSTRUMENTS

Nephoscope

A nephoscope is used to detect the wind direction at cloud height. It can be made with small pieces of scrap wood, glue, a round mirror, and dark paint.

1. Cut a wood base for mounting the mirror.
2. Glue the mirror to the center of the wood base.
3. Mark compass directions around edge of mirror and paint a cross mark in the center of the mirror.
4. Orient the nephoscope with a compass; align the north mark on the indicator with the north mark on the compass.
5. Place the nephoscope on the ground and follow a cloud as it passes over the center of the mirror until it reaches the edge.
6. Note the direction the cloud is moving toward. If it is blowing toward the east, the wind is coming from the west.

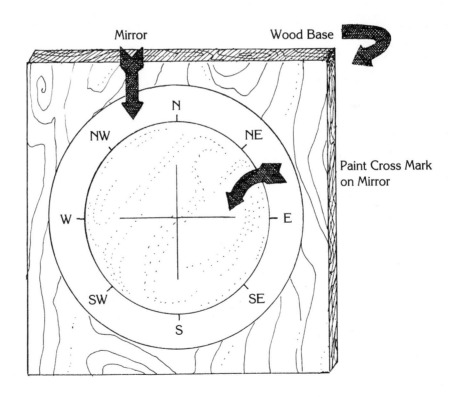

Mirror   Wood Base

Paint Cross Mark on Mirror

Science

Anemometer An anemometer is used to measure wind speed in revolutions per minute (rpm). It can be made with four small cones from a drinking fountain (3″ × 5″ cards can be substituted for these—see below); a piece of cardboard (6 cm × 6 cm); one nail (#16, 3 1/2 inch); one plastic soda straw (6-cm-long piece); one wooden or cardboard base (three thicknesses of cardboard glued together or heavy cardboard), 10 cm × 10 cm; scissors; glue; scotch tape.

1. Cut a 6-cm cardboard square and draw two diagonal lines.

   Where the diagonals intersect, punch a hole with the nail. Enlarge it until the straw fits snugly in the hole.

 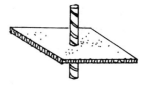

   Cut four slots in the cone holder as shown below (cut in 1–2 centimeters).

2. Slide a cone into each slot. Be sure they all face the same direction (clockwise or counter-clockwise).

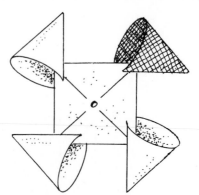

Mark the cone holder with a reference point (or color one of the cones) to help count revolutions.

Run the nail through the straw and tap it into the base (you may want to put a washer here).

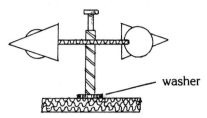

If cones are not available, take a 3″ × 5″ card and fold it as shown below:

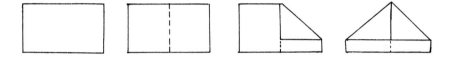

Tape it with scotch tape. Cut on a curve as shown in the drawing. Then open the cone.

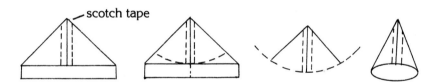

The anemometer determines wind speed. Wind speeds are reported in revolutions per minute. Using a digital watch or a watch with a sweep second hand, have one student say "Go!" and keep time. Have another student count how many times the colored cone or marker goes by. After a minute (or fraction of a minute), the time keeper says "Stop!" and the other student reports how many times the colored cone or marker went by.

Most of the copy and illustrations on pages 134–136 are taken directly from *Terrestrial Hi-Lo* (© 1975, The Regents of the University of California), a unit from the *Outdoor Biology Instructional Strategies* (OBIS) curriculum developed at the Lawrence Hall of Science at the University of California, Berkeley.

Science

Wind Vane

A wind vane is used to determine wind direction. It can be made using one piece of heavy-duty aluminum foil (15 cm × 2 cm); one nail (#16, 3 1/2 inch); one plastic soda straw (6-cm-long piece); scissors; glue; scotch tape; one wooden or cardboard base, 10 cm × 10 cm (see directions for anemometer).

1. Cut a piece of the aluminum foil 15 cm × 2 cm. Bend this around the piece of straw as shown below.

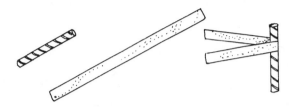

2. Fold the pieces of aluminum foil tightly and tape them together near the straw. Tape the foil to the straw to prevent it from sliding up and down.

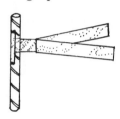

3. Put the nail through the straw and tap it into the base. Spread the two pieces of aluminum foil slightly.

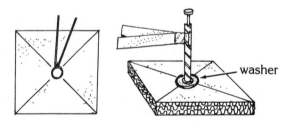

washer

Wind direction is named for the direction it comes from. A wind blowing from the south is a south wind. A compass is useful to determine exact geographic locations. See the social studies chapter for other techniques used to establish direction.

Options and Extensions

You may want to do this before the weather study. Data collection can be introduced and practiced by distributing a package of M & M's to groups of 2 or 3 students after dividing the class into thirds. Then have groups complete the data chart as shown below. Ask students to form observations and inferences from their data.

M & M Data Analysis

Color	I. Number of each color in your small group's package	II. Totals of each color for your large group	III. Average number of each color for your large group	IV. Total number of each color for the class	V. Average number of each color for the class
Orange					
Yellow					
Green					
Tan					
Brown					

(Adapted from *Arithmetic Teacher,* January, 1978.)

Ask students to report on this weather study by writing a paragraph or two on the problems or difficulties they had with collecting the weather data and analyzing it.

Invite a meteorologist to talk to the class about data collection and interpretation for specific geographic locations.

Science

Notes on the use of Science Beyond the Classroom activities:

Discovering the Community

"... education is in constant process of invention."

Jerome Bruner

Each community—village, town, suburb, city—has myriad resources that you and students can use to make curriculum come to life and the learning process more relevant. Discovering the history of a village cemetery, exploring the excitement of a nearby woods, studying the mysteries of a town's stream, or recording information about a particular neighborhood are a few examples of the community resources discussed in this chapter.

A common denominator throughout this chapter is the thinking skills approach to learning. Observing, measuring, classifying, inferring, communicating are emphasized. In the forest study, for example, groups of students are encouraged to focus on cross sections of logs, to list observations, and then to make inferences and interpretations. In the stream investigation, students are shown how to measure stream flow, to index organisms, to determine water quality, and finally to organize and communicate their findings.

The eight activities presented in this chapter barely scratch the surface of the available community resources. A nearby swamp or bog, an abandoned farm, a beach, an old one-room schoolhouse—the list could go on indefinitely. We hope that the chapter's activities and methods will serve as models for those of you who are searching for exciting ways to use their own community resources and enhance school curriculum.

The Lot Next Door

Purpose

To identify a vacant lot's characteristics and the community's use of it and to observe the plants and animals that live there; to learn the history of the vacant lot and the community's feelings toward it.

Description

Students are introduced to a vacant lot and study its setting, size, and history. Students then look at the variety of living organisms found there and their adaptation to this environment. Finally, they study the history of the lot, researching what its uses have been in the past and the natural changes it is undergoing. A clean-up of the lot and a junk art project can be done if needed.

Materials

Part 1: drawing paper, pencil, crayons, camera.
Part 2: notebook, pencil, manila paper, crayons.
Part 3: several sheets of newsprint, marking pens, a large piece of tagboard.
Part 4: notebook, pencil, envelope, stamp, books, magazines, periodicals (a trip to the local library may be necessary).
Part 5: notebook, pencil, camera.
Part 6: pencil, alphabet diversity hike worksheet.
Part 7: collecting bags and boxes, glue, scissors, hammer, nails, string, stapler, camera, collected junk.

Process

**Part 1:
Introduction to
the Physical
Setting**

At the beginning of the school year, introduce students to the vacant lot. Visit the lot, walk around it and talk about what is observed.

Have each student (or student team) select a different area and make a drawing of it. A plot 12 feet square is suggested.

Have a class photographer record views of each plot on film so that the student drawings can be validated.

Upon completion of the drawings, have the class return to school and discuss their findings. This discussion might include the following questions:

1. Why is the lot vacant?
2. What does it do to and for the community?
3. What survives on the lot and how does it survive?
4. Does the lot have beauty in its present state?

**Part 2:
Adaptation
of Organisms**

A classroom discussion of adaptation as it relates to the plants and animals in the city is necessary so that the students know what they are looking for at the site. Students should have the following list of questions to work with while recording the data:

Community

1. What animals and plants do you see on the lot?
2. What animals and plants are most abundant?
3. What kind of ecological relationship exists between the animals and plants?
4. How do the animals escape from their enemies?
5. Where do the animals sleep, nest, or hide from their enemies or the elements?

Have students keep a record of the plant and animal life observed during a half-hour period.

Plant Life

Devising a key identifying the different plant types found on a vacant lot will graphically show all the kinds of plants located in each plot. The student team searches its own designated area and selects one sample of each type of plant. These plants can be taped to a large sheet of paper which is centrally located. Have the student that brought the first sample of each plant type invent and draw a symbol on a chart to represent each plant identified. This then becomes a reference (key) for future work: choosing one plant and examining the variations between specimens; comparing the number of one species of plant; mapping plant types; showing succession and seasonal change.

A variety of plant types will probably be found. Possibilities:

clover	foxtail	dandelion
plantain	yellow goat's beard	lamb's quarters
oxalis	wild grasses	wild rhubarb
white campion	goldenrod	wild carrot
climbing nightshade	shepherd's purse	milkweed
deadly nightshade	thistle	pigweed

Other plants that might also be found are seedlings from trees surrounding the lot and domestic flowers that have escaped from gardens. As a special project, students could use a handbook to make a plant key. One such handbook is *Spotter's Guide to Wild Flowers of North America*, Mayflower Books, New York, 1979.

Animal Life

The students should check the plot for signs of small and large animal life—burrows, droppings, nests, and tracks. Encourage students to look around fences and trees; under cement blocks and large stones; in hollows and banks; under vegetation.

Have students record and map their findings. The majority of animal life found will be insects or other "bugs." A key similar to the one done for plant life can be done to help students focus on specific details.

After returning to the classroom, have students share and discuss their findings. Then have them draw pictures of and write about a make-believe animal that could survive on the lot. The animal must eat something on the lot; have parts of its body adapted to finding and eating this food; be able to escape from other animals or protect itself; be able to obtain water.

Share the drawings and stories and discuss plant and animal adaptation as a means of survival.

Part 3: Interdependence of Life

Nothing can survive on its own, and the most basic requirement is food. In the previous lesson, adaptation to the vacant lot was discussed. Using the data from that lesson, a food chain can be developed showing the interdependence of plant and animal life on the vacant lot.

Review the data collected from the previous lesson, pointing out the source of food of the various animals and plants observed. On newsprint, trace the food source of one animal. For example, an insect eats plants, plants derive nutrients from water and soil, animal and plant waste return to the soil. Do this for several different animals.

Develop a "vacant lot food chain" chart for a number of the animals. Once the chart is complete, discuss the effects of a break in the food chain. Help students understand what might happen if the chain is broken.

Part 4: A History of the Lot

Over the years, many changes have taken place in the vacant lot. By determining the history of the lot, these changes can be inferred. Have students brainstorm ways of gathering information about past uses of the lot.

Have students write letters to various city departments, to newspapers, and to the historical society and plan interviews. Have groups of students cover a 40- to 50-year period starting at 1800 (or any date you feel is appropriate).

Have each group report its findings to the class. The information can be compiled in a scrap book, a chart, or some other suitable way.

Part 5: Natural Changes the Lot Is Undergoing

Natural changes have also taken place on the lot. These changes can be seasonal, the result of severe weather, or the result of day-to-day occurrences. The more closely the lot is observed, the more evident these changes will be to the class.

Since this unit can span the whole school year, seasonal changes can be observed and recorded with regular visits to the lot. The class can see which plants and animals survive, determine why they survive, and see what changes occur in them. Results should be recorded in some predetermined fashion.

Severe weather will also cause change. After a rainstorm or snowstorm, point out the effects of the weather on the plant and animal life in the lot. Encourage the students to look for ground cracks, erosion, broken branches, and so on.

Part 6:
Diversity on
the Vacant Lot

A diverse environment is a healthy environment. When land becomes polluted, displacement occurs, and only those animals that can adapt to the new conditions survive; the others die off or move. Many of the survivors are pests and weeds.

Have students go on an Alphabet Diversity Hike to the lot. Divide them into groups. Have each group alphabetically list as many man-made and natural things as they can find.

After completing the hike, the lack of diversity, particularly among the natural items, should be evident when the lists are shared.

Plan a second hike to a wooded area, a park, or country setting. Use the same method of gathering data and compare the results.

Alphabet Diversity Hike

Natural	Man-made
A. _____	A. _____
B. _____	B. _____
C. _____	C. _____
↓	↓
T. _____	T. _____

Part 7:
Improving the
Environment

If the vacant lot has become a dumping ground for the neighborhood, the class may decide to clean it up (an excellent community action project). A junk art activity can be included to add interest to the project. The following steps are suggested for a junk sculpture or a junk collage.

Have the class go to the lot and begin picking up objects. Working in groups, they can decide which things are appropriate for the art project and which things should be discarded.

After the clean-up is complete, have the class photographer take pictures of the clean lot.

Upon returning to the classroom, lay out the collected junk so that the students can look over what is available for constructing their projects. Demonstrate several methods of assembling the junk so that it will stay together, then have students begin to assemble their own projects. Stress creativity and the concept that sculpture is three-dimensional.

Once the projects are complete, have the class critique the project based on the aesthetic merits—of junk sculpture, the sculptors' creativity, and the ingenuity of assembly.

Options and
Extensions

Contact local historians or senior citizens who know the area. Invite them to share their experiences of the area with the class. This will help reinforce the sense of history of the vacant lot and of the community as a whole.

Archaeology Adventure

Purpose
To experience directly the work of an archaeologist, to collect and classify site material, to interpret the past events of a specific environment.

Description
Students visit a dig in the community: the remains of a foundry, the foundation of a glass works, a deserted farm, an abandoned house, an old landfill. They collect and classify objects, survey the environment for former land use, and formulate ideas of past life styles.

Materials
Clipboard, paper, pencil, collection boxes and bags.

Process
Discuss the site to be visited and kinds of artifacts the students can anticipate finding. Design a classification system for the visit. If, for example, a foundation of an old factory is explored, the students could classify finds as they relate to the factory's physical plant, tools, manufactured goods, packaging, shipping, and so on. Students could also focus on the factors contributing to the factory's specific location: population, transportation, and terrain.

After the site visit, give students an opportunity to share their finds and interpretations. Outline questions for the class to research: "What factors contributed to the factory's closing?" and "What impact did the initial opening and then the closing of the factory have on the community?"

Options and Extensions
Have students locate and interview senior citizens who were involved with the site and visit local newspaper archives.

Community

Indian Craft Outing

Purpose   To identify and gather natural craft materials, to make simple Indian tools and crafts, and to appreciate the American Indian's reverence for the environment.

Description   Students select a number of Indian crafts, gather natural materials from various settings, and make samples of these Indian crafts.

Materials   Clippers, scissors, collection bags, thread, needle, crock (for clay), drill-bits.

Process   Have students list various Indian crafts they would enjoy learning—stringing necklaces, making headbands, making pottery, weaving mats, and so on. Divide the class into groups according to the crafts selected. Have each group identify the natural materials needed for their craft and the environment in which these materials may be found—woods, field, stream, pond, schoolyard. For example, a group may choose to weave small mats out of cattail reeds and grasses and identify a swampy area near the school where these materials can be found. Another group may decide to make necklaces and choose to use nut shells and pine cones from the woods nearby. Encourage the groups to help each other by sharing information on areas where the materials can be found.

Plan field trips to gather the necessary natural materials or help the groups organize to collect the materials on their own. Have students return to the classroom to share their findings and make the crafts. Finally, discuss how the Indians' use of natural materials exhibited a reverence for their surroundings.

Options and Extensions   Plan a field trip to a natural history museum to see displays of Indian crafts. Invite a natural crafts enthusiast in to share experiences and projects.

How Are You, Neighbor?

Purpose

To study the neighborhood as an environment, focusing on the interaction of persons, places, and things; to be aware of the out-of-doors in an urban setting; and to learn how the natural and man-made environments co-exist.

Description

Students concentrate on the environment that is most familiar to them: the neighborhood community. Places, things, and how people interact with them are all part of the students' experience. This activity will help make the students more aware of how their neighborhood is changing, why their neighborhood is changing, how much they depend on the neighborhood and its services, and how they relate to their neighborhood.

Materials

Notebook or clipboard, paper, pencil, worksheets, crayons, large drawing paper, rulers, city maps (if available).

Process

Part 1: Becoming Aware

Introduce the word *environment* and ask the class what it means to them. After discussion, take the class on a walking field trip to a particular environment: the neighborhood. Have students identify the boundaries of the neighborhood and work in small groups to complete the information sheet on page 148.

1. Name the buildings in the area that are most interesting, most important, oldest, smallest, largest, most beautiful, and ugliest.

	Name	Use
Most interesting	_____	_____
	_____	_____
	_____	_____
Most Important	_____	_____
	_____	_____
Oldest	_____	_____
	_____	_____
Smallest	_____	_____
	_____	_____
Largest	_____	_____
	_____	_____
Most Beautiful	_____	_____
	_____	_____
Ugliest	_____	_____
	_____	_____

2. What material is used in the construction of the houses and buildings?
3. How old would you estimate the houses and buildings to be? What clues led you to this estimate?
4. How many streets are in the area? What kinds of streets (lanes, alleys, and so on) are included? What materials were used in their construction? Are there many differences?
5. What types of public and private services are available in the neighborhood? How many of them have you and your family used?

**Part 2:
Finding Out
More**

Divide the class into six groups. Have them work independently on the following projects and report their findings to the class.

Group I—Have this group research the number and types of dwellings found in the neighborhood. Ask them to prepare a report on living styles, using the following list as a guide.

One family	High rise
Two family	Low income (CMHA, FHA, HUD)
Duplex	Row house
Condominium or townhouse	Ranch style
Colonial	Split level
Bungalow	Mobile home
Apartment	Old mansion or century home

Group II—Have students concentrate on open spaces found in the area. Have them include the names and locations of streets, parking lots, vacant lots, playing fields, and parks. Then ask them to plot these places on a map (or prepare a sketch) and describe them.

Group III—Have this group study the different types of materials used in the building industry. Have them prepare an illustrated handout for the class and include the following building materials in the report. Ask students to find out whether the materials are manufactured or processed locally.

Brick	Tile
Aluminum siding	Cement
Wood (frame construction)	Concrete
Stone (kinds, how used)	

Community

Group IV—Have this group research different sensory impressions, listing neighborhood sounds, smells, and colors and discussing their findings. Some examples are given below.

Sound	Smell	Color
Traffic	Fresh cut grass	Green lawn
Police siren	Smoke	Blue sky
Barking dogs	Donut shop	Gray clouds
Rain	Barbecue	Gray gravel
Thunder		Red flowers
Vendors		
Children playing		
Rustling leaves		
Church bells		

Finally, have students pinpoint sensory impressions that are unique to their neighborhood and discuss why these responses might make the neighborhood different from other neighborhoods.

Group V—Have students make a list of the kinds of people they are accustomed to seeing in the neighborhood.

Residents	Nonresidents
Small children	Mail carrier
Teenagers	Police officer
Old people	Friends of residents
Young people	Meter reader
Men	Delivery truck driver
Women	Door-to-door salesperson
Musicians, punk rockers	Garbage collector
Others (describe them)	Others (describe them)

Have students pinpoint the kind of people most prevalent in the neighborhood and how they influence it.

Group VI—Have this group list the kinds of things they like to do and classify the activities in the following categories:

Activities done in the neighborhood	Activities done outside the neighborhood
Visit friends	Go to concerts
Visit playground	See movies
Garden	Shop
Give parties	Hike
Walk in the park	Ice skate
Roller skate	Visit YMCA or YWCA
Others (describe them)	Others (describe them)

Encourage students to brainstorm ideas for how to bring some of the outside activities into the neighborhood.

In addition to making a report to the class, have each group write a story about the neighborhood. The stories may describe a family in the neighborhood, an incident in the neighborhood, or a day in the life of someone who lives in the neighborhood.

The plots should include information from all the reports. The names may be fictitious, but the neighborhood must be portrayed accurately. Have students read the stories to the rest of the class.

Options and Extensions

Major changes—roads being built, buildings being torn down, and houses being built—are easy to see in our environment. However, unless a major earth-moving piece of equipment comes into the schoolyard, students are often not aware of changes taking place right in front of them. Have them spend a week keeping track of changes they see taking place around one part of the city; for example, this side of the bridge, or south of a particular street. At the end of the week, discuss students' findings and see if they are surprised by how much they noticed.

Community

Forest Focus

Purpose   To develop an awareness of the forces at work in a forest environment, to visualize the life cycles of trees, to sense the interrelatedness of a forest community, to elicit questions about the forest through a sensory awareness and thinking skills investigation.

Description   Students are led through a variety of activities that combine specific concepts with sensory awareness experiences. Students with partners or in small groups focus on the forest floor, trees, rotting stumps, and other natural materials to learn about the forest environment.

Materials   Blindfold, art paper (8″ × 11″), clipboard, soil samples, forest litter (dead leaves, nuts, pinecones), decayed wood and log cross sections.

Process   Use all or a few of the following activities in large or small blocks of time to investigate the forest environment.

Part 1: Log Cross Section Experience   Prior to visiting a wooded area have students in small groups examine log cross sections, listing observations—number of rings, grain pattern, blemishes or stains, bark color and texture—and then make interpretations or inferences about what has been observed. Encourage students to formulate and share their questions: What do the rings represent? How fast do trees grow? Why do some trees grow faster than others? Why are some rings farther apart than others?

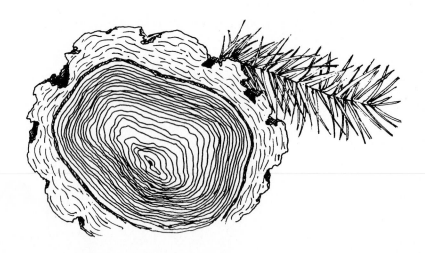

Part 2:
Rotten Log or
Stump
Experience

Have small groups of students visit a wooded area and locate rotten logs or stumps. Have each group focus on what things are changing the rotten stump.

Living Things	Effects on Stump
Nonliving Things	Effects on Stump

After the groups have had opportunity to make observations and inferences, have them visit each other's stumps and share answers to the following questions: What things about the stump give us clues about past events? What factors caused these things to happen?

Part 3:
Tree Exploration

Have students choose partners. One partner is blindfolded and led through a small area of woods. Students without blindfolds select trees for their partners to become acquainted with. Those with blindfolds describe what they are sensing: the size of tree's trunk, the bark's texture and smell, unusual markings of tree's surface, size and shape of the lower branches, positioning and size of exposed roots.

Following the exploration, partners return to a central location that is not too far from the trees. Students remove blindfolds, describe their trees again and then attempt to locate them. After each partner has had opportunity to experience being blindfolded, have the class come together and share their observations and perceptions. Focus on what new discoveries have been made about trees and the forest.

Part 4:
Touch of Color

While visiting a wooded area, pass out paper to the class and have each student, using natural materials (soil, berries, flowers, leaves, moss), draw a picture of the forest setting. Give the class an opportunity to display their work and describe their feelings about the surroundings. Encourage the students to discuss what materials were used to add color.

**Part 5:
Life Line
of a Tree**

Ask small groups of students to examine closely a number of objects from a tree. These might include the following:

seedlings of various sizes	nuts
log cross sections	pine cones
small branches	leaves
chunks of decaying wood	peat
forest soil	

Encourage the students to share their observations and discoveries with each other. After a few minutes ask, "What do all these materials have in common?" Next, have the class work together and place all the objects in a sequence that represents a tree's life line. Some groups may end up making a life cycle. Have the students explain the rationale for the order of materials in the life line. Then discuss some of the following questions: Do the life lines of all trees follow the same pattern? What are some ways a tree's life line can be altered? What other materials could be included in the life line? How many years might a tree's life line represent?

Finally, hike through a forested area and have the students share together their observations on the different stages of the life lines of trees they see around them.

**Options and
Extensions**

Invite a forester to discuss work, training, and career opportunities with the class.

Mysteries for a Cemetery Sleuth

Purpose
To use the cemetery as a resource for teaching the school curriculum, to appreciate a cemetery as part of the general ecology and history of an area, to identify feelings and clarify values about this common human landmark.

Description
Students conduct a cemetery investigation by working in small groups using the following four-step plan:

1. Identify approaches to a cemetery study, including subject areas and kinds of activities that could form the basis for the investigation.
2. Develop a plan of action based on the results obtained in step 1.
3. Conduct a field investigation of a cemetery using the methods of collecting, recording, and interpreting data.
4. Communicate the cemetery investigation findings by planning a report that focuses on the methods used and the information collected.

Materials
Notebook or clipboard, paper, pencil, worksheets, crayons, ruler, yardstick or meter stick, charcoal, chalk, sheets of newsprint, magnifying glass, topographical map of area, camera.

Process
To prepare for this activity, submit an outline of the scope and objectives of the project for support and approval of the school administration. Contact local authorities (police and cemetery owners) to obtain permission to use the grounds. Also, find out any special rules concerning their use. If a small historical cemetery is nearby, it would seem to be the best choice.

Send permission slips home with students, enumerating date, time, location, supervision, and nature of the field trip (see the following suggested form letter).

Dear _____(Parent or Guardian)_____

Our class will soon begin a unit of study on ____(cemetery name)____ cemetery. This cemetery is an interdisciplinary resource offering a wide variety of activities in the areas of social studies, math, art, science, and language arts.

Much of our study will be done at the cemetery. Therefore, we will be taking a number of ____(means of transportation)____ field trips to this location, and some parent assistance will be needed. Permission to use the property has been obtained from local authorities and school officials have approved the trip.

We need help from descendants of persons buried at ____(cemetery name)____ and resource persons for genealogy, headstone rubbing, and local history. If you can help in any of these areas, please indicate below. Thank you.

Sincerely,

- -

My son/daughter _____ has permission to go on any field trips pertaining to the cemetery study unit. Tentative dates, depending on weather conditions, are ____(dates and times)____ .

I can accompany one field trip.   Yes ____ No ____

I have a book you can borrow.   Yes ____ No ____

I can help in this way: _____

- -

Before conducting the cemetery study, identify student feelings toward the cemetery by discussing the following questions:

When you think of a cemetery, what kinds of feelings and attitudes come to your mind? (Make a list of these and save for discussion at the end of the investigation.)

How many of these attitudes and feelings have you actually experienced yourself, and how many come from books, movies, or friends? Which ones are true? How do you know they are?

Have the class brainstorm the kinds of activities in the various subject areas that could be included in a cemetery study. If the cemetery is very large, smaller areas within it can be marked off with string. The following list of suggested subject area activities is included to help you guide the discussion.

Mathematics

1. Calculate the ages of all the people in the cemetery.

2. Place the ages of the people on a distribution chart. Is any pattern evident? Do you have a lot of deaths in one year? Were there any epidemics or disasters that year? Who is the oldest person in the cemetery? Who is the youngest? Are more older than younger? Graph the number of people with the same year of death. Did more people die in the 1800s to 1850s, the 1850s to 1900s, the 1900s to 1950s, or the 1950s to the 1970s?

3. Analyze the data in terms of the statistic that women live longer than men.

4. Map the distribution of graves in the cemetery. Is one section of the cemetery older? Is the cemetery arranged alphabetically? Are there family plots? Are any graves separated by chain or fences?

5. Identify and draw geometric shapes of the various tombstones. Is there one that is more common than the others? What might be the reasons for this?

6. Pace off and draw a map of the cemetery indicating positions of gravestones (devise a scale and transfer dimensions to graph paper).

Social Studies

1. Make a census of the cemetery. Record all the names and do a profile of ethnic groups. Construct family trees.

2. Study the early pioneers in your area who may be buried in the cemetery. Sources of information include town histories, biographies, old maps, photographs, private letters, interviews with senior citizens, diaries, newspapers, and public records. Try to trace families only from the stones. Look for name changes through marriage.

3. Compile a list of all the occupations discovered from the stones. How have occupations changed?

4. Research the lives of the famous people buried in the cemetery. What evidence of historical events can be seen in the cemetery? How many soldiers are buried in the cemetery? In which wars did they fight?

5. Determine the cemetery's location in relationship to the community.

Language Arts

1. Make a list of the epitaphs from the cemetery (poems or facts about the person buried there). Is any one poem used more than once? What does the epitaph tell you about the person? What does it tell you about how others felt about that person? Cause of death can sometimes be learned from the epitaph. Can you tell this from any of the epitaphs written in this cemetery?

2. List first names that are unfamiliar to you.

3. Take a few pictures of parts of the cemetery that interest you. Write a poem about one picture or a group of them.

4. List changes in language patterns and styles. Notice the spelling of the various names. Do you detect any changes in spelling?

Science

1. Identify the different types of tombstones in the cemetery. Are there any unusual ones? Tombstones are made from many different materials: granite, sandstone, slate, glass, wood, and combinations of these. Observe the effects of weathering of the stones. Which stones seem to have weathered faster? Does location make a difference? Are more weathered stones found in an open area or surrounded by trees or bushes?

2. Describe the landscaping of the cemetery. Are there many flowers, plants, shrubs, or trees? Can you identify them? Is the cemetery well kept? Look around the cemetery for some large trees. Measure the circumference of these trees. Do these measurements give you any indication to the age of the cemetery? What do you notice about the soil conditions? If possible, get a soil sample to analyze.

3. Draw a rough topographic map indicating elevations, depressions, and other special land features. Note unusual ecological conditions, such as poor drainage or erosion.

Art

1. Sketch the different styles of tombstones in the cemetery. Does any one style or design seem more prevalent?

2. Make some tombstone rubbings. Not only can rubbings help you decipher some of the stones that are harder to read, but they also make unique art work. This can be done with lightweight paper or tissue paper and the side of an old crayon or charcoal. Various lettering styles can be rubbed. Research the type of lettering and its period of history.

3. Compare and contrast the varying styles of sculpture.

4. Find evidence of beauty and color and describe your observations.

5. Fold an 11 × 18 sheet of paper in half. On one side, draw a grave marker as it appears today. On the other half of the paper draw how you think the grave marker will appear in 100 years.

Divide the class into small groups and have each group develop a plan of action for investigating one or two of the activities suggested. Each group should consider how to divide responsibilities, what information to collect, efficient ways to collect and record information, and supplies and equipment needed.

Conduct a field investigation of a cemetery using the methods developed by each small group. A sample data sheet is included below.

Cemetery Investigation

Name	Year of Birth	Year of Death	Age	Type of Grave Marker	Miscellaneous Information

Group the ages of the people whose names you recorded:

0–10 _____	51–60 _____
11–20 _____	61–70 _____
21–30 _____	71–80 _____
31–40 _____	81–90 _____
41–50 _____	91–100 _____

During what period did most people die?

18th Century _____

19th Century _____

20th Century _____

What are some possible reasons for the previous finding?

_____

_____

_____

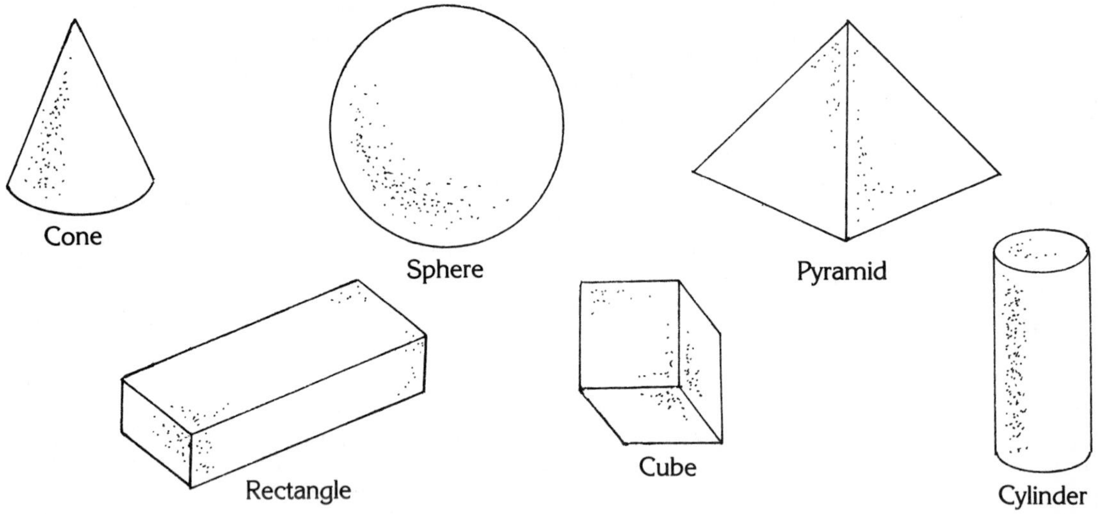

Cone

Sphere

Pyramid

Rectangle

Cube

Cylinder

Draw a sketch of a gravestone that is made up of at least two of the shapes above.

Draw a sketch of the gravestone of which you made a rubbing.

Stone Type	Tally	Number	Color	Decorations	Weathered
Granite					
Marble					
Limestone					
Cement					
Other					

What types of stones seem to last the longest? _____

_____

What evidence did you find of epidemics, plagues, wars, or catastrophes in the community? _____

_____

What section of the cemetery seems to have the oldest graves?

_____

Epitaph   Poetic Example: _____

_____

_____

Satirical Example: _____

_____

_____

  After returning from the cemetery, students should be given time to meet with their groups and compile information. Additional preparation time may be required to do research in the library and the community. Each member of the group should participate in the presentation. Each group should use visual displays. Have each group consider what they did, how they did it, and what it meant.

  Each group should be allowed approximately 15–20 minutes to share their experiences with the rest of the class. A discussion of findings and opinions should follow the presentations.

Have the students again think about their feelings and attitudes toward the cemetery. Make a list and have them compare it to the original one completed at the beginning of the study. Encourage the students to share new feelings.

Follow-up activities can be as extensive as you and the class desire, depending on interest level and capabilities.

Options and Extensions

Have students write their epitaphs or poems, haiku, or short stories using the cemetery as a theme. Research tombstones. There are many different styles of tombstones. The designs are symbols that can be traced to biblical times. Changes in belief about death can also be researched in the style of stones. Invite local historians to share their knowledge and information about the community and its descendants.

Some Suggested Reference Books

Jacobs, G. Walker. *Stranger Stop and Cast an Eye: A Guide to Gravestones and Gravestone Rubbing*. Brattleboro, Vt.: Stephen Green Press, 1973.

Kull, Andrew. *New England Cemeteries: A Collector's Guide*. Brattleboro, Vt.: Stephen Green Press, 1975.

Mann, Thomas, and Janet Greene. *Over Their Dead Bodies: Yankee Epitaphs and History*. Brattleboro, Vt.: Stephen Green Press, 1962.

Provenzo, Asterie Baker, and Eugene B. Provenzo. *Pursuing the Past: Oral History, Photographs, Family History, Cemeteries*. Menlo Park, Calif.: Addison-Wesley Publishing Company, Inc., 1984.

Smith, Joseph L. *Tombs, Temples, and Ancient Art*. Norman, Okla.: University of Oklahoma Press, 1956.

Stream Search

Purpose

To investigate the physical characteristics of a stream, to observe the different habitats and relationships associated with the stream, to determine the water quality of a stream by using a biotic index and chemical analysis.

Description

Students explore the general characteristics of a stream, including its source, watershed, major physical features, stream flow, temperatures, and pH readings. Students also relate their personal reflections, awarenesses, and values about the stream and its surroundings. Finally, students determine the health of a stream by collecting and classifying organisms according to their ability to tolerate pollution and by measuring the amount of oxygen in the water.

Materials

Notebook or clipboard, pencil, worksheets, white dishpans, oxygen content water test kit, kitchen strainer, hand lens, tweezers, baby food jars, 50 ft. or 100 ft. tape measure, thermometer, topographic map of quadrangle, litmus paper, watch, corks.

**Process
Part 1: Topo
Map Survey of a
Stream and Its
Watershed**

Show the class a topographic map of the quad in which you will be doing the stream study. Locate the stream and point out familiar landmarks. The class should practice reading the topo map. The following exercise is suggested to acquaint them with a topo map's characteristics.

Interpreting a Topographic Map

A topographic map locates both man-made and natural features in an area called a quadrangle. Man-made features are indicated by specific symbols. The one feature indicated by a topographic map that is not shown on any other type of map is the physical characteristics of the terrain. These characteristics include the elevation as well as location of mountains, valleys, plains, streams, and rivers.

The elevation is usually measured in feet and is recorded as the number of feet above sea level.

In order to be able to indicate elevation, topographic maps use a symbol called a <u>contour line.</u> A contour line connects all points that are at the same elevation. The <u>contour interval</u> is the vertical difference in feet between each contour line. Every fourth or fifth contour line is usually marked with a numerical value, which indicates the distance above sea level. The following is an example of how contour lines appear on a map.

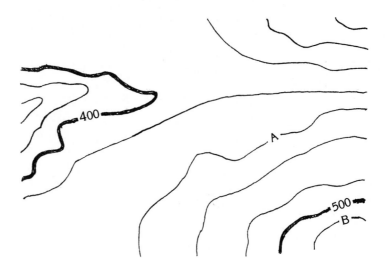

Answer the following questions:

1. What is the thick line with the 400 written in it called? _____

2. What is the contour interval of the above map?

   _____

3. What is the elevation at line A? _____

4. What is the elevation at line B? _____

5. When traveling from line A to line B, are you going up or down? _____

Water Flow and the Topographic Map

All bodies of water are indicated in blue on a topographic map. A contour line bends upstream when crossing a valley. Quite often the valley will have a stream at its bottom. The ground must rise away from the stream's course.

The inside of a closed contour line is the high side unless it is hachured (see point A on the map below). If the line is hachured, it is at the same elevation as the contour line before it. The next hachured line is one contour interval below the first hachured line. Actually, all contour lines are closed, but since the area covered by a map is limited, the point at which the contour lines meet is often not on the map.

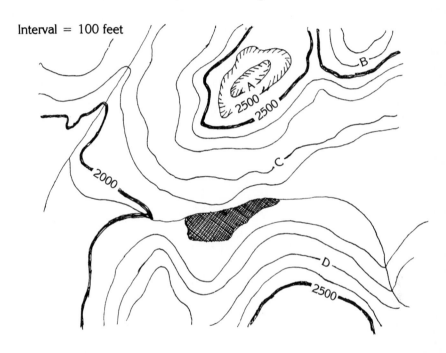

Interval = 100 feet

Answer the following questions:

1. What is the elevation at contour line A? _____

2. What is the elevation at contour line B? _____

3. What is the elevation at contour line C? _____

4. What is the elevation at contour line D? _____

5. What is the elevation of the lake? _____

6. Draw an arrow indicating the direction of flow of each of the streams.

Watershed is the term used to describe the land area that drains into the stream being studied. In order to help the students understand a watershed, have them complete the following activity.

Watershed and Water Quality

Watershed is the term used to describe all the land area that drains into a specific stream, river, or lake. The water may move on the soil as run-off or in the soil as ground water. The size of a watershed may vary from a few hundred yards to several hundred square miles.

Most of the water that people use spends some time in or on the watershed. If the watershed is made of soils that will not allow the water to sink in, a summer shower could cause a flash flood. If, on the other hand, the watershed is made of soils that are highly porous, you have an ideal place for sinking a well. Materials such as fertilizers, pesticides, animal wastes, industrial wastes can and do enter the ground water. This ground water, which is tapped by wells, can also run off into the streams, rivers, and lakes, decreasing the quality of the water. The water quality can become so poor that it cannot be used.

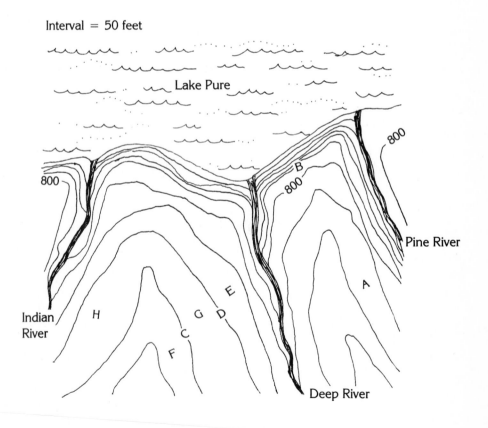

Answer the following questions:

1. What is the first body of water that a raindrop falling at point A would enter as run-off?
2. Which body of water on the map would this drop of water finally enter?
3. What is the first body of water that a raindrop falling at point B would enter as run-off?
4. What soil condition would prevent the drop of water at point A from entering the ground water?
5. Why do communities have to build storm sewers (sewers that carry rain water?)
6. Where is the most likely place for a storm sewer to empty if it starts at point H?
7. If all the land at point G between contour lines C and D does not allow water to sink into it, what is likely to happen to a home at point E during a rainstorm?
8. A company discharges sulfuric acid onto the soil at point G. You wish to build a new home and have the choice of buying property at either point E or F. Both places would require you to dig a well for water. Which property would you buy? What reasons did you use to make your choice?

Other questions for your class to answer using a topo map:

1. What is the watershed for the school?
2. What rivers or streams form the watershed?
3. How can the topo map help predict water quality?

Part 2: Stream Awareness

Have the students describe their thoughts, feelings, and attitudes about a stream in a descriptive paragraph and a charcoal or pencil drawing.

Nature's symphony can be experienced by the class as they sit next to a stream and concentrate on the various sounds around them. The students can express their reflections on this symphony through poetry using the *cinquain, nouning,* or *haiku* format.

Cinquain

Title in two syllables
Description of title in four syllables
Action in six syllables
Expression of feeling in eight syllables
Another word for the title in two syllables

Nouning

Noun title
Two adjectives
Three verbs
Phrase
Repeat noun

Haiku

Three lines of
5 syllables
7 syllables
5 syllables

Using only the colors and materials provided by nature (leaves, twigs, flowers, bark), have students paint a picture of the stream and part of its surroundings.

Part 3: Stream Physical Features

Have several students draw a map of the stream 50 meters upstream and downstream from a point of entry, indicating major features in the stream—pools, riffles, large rocks, and feeder streams. Show major features on the bank—roads, rocks, trails, trees, logs. Mark with a symbol where each remaining team is working.

Have several students record air and water temperatures, taking the surface temperature at one-meter intervals across the stream. Next, take the temperature at the bottom near the shore and then in the center of the stream. Record the air temperature on the bank and on each side of the stream near its edge. Record all the readings on a data sheet (a sample form is provided at the end of this section). On page 169 is a chart showing water temperature ranges and their relationship to the growth of certain organisms.

Temperature Ranges (Approximate) Required for Growth of Certain Organisms

Temperature		Examples of life
Greater than 68°		Much plant life; many fish diseases; most bass, crappie, bluegill, carp, catfish; caddisfly.
Less than 68°	Upper range (55°–68°)	Some plant life; some fish diseases; salmon, trout; stonefly, mayfly, caddisfly, water beetles, striders.
	Lower range (Less than 55°)	Trout; caddisfly, stonefly, mayfly.

Have students determine the pH at the same measurement locations used for water temperature. These readings are to be recorded on the data sheet. The following chart indicates the relationship between various pH ranges and aquatic life.

pH Ranges That Support Aquatic Life

Most Acid					Neutral						Most Alkaline		
1	2	3	4	5	6	7	8	9	10	11	12	13	14

bacteria
1.0 _____ 13.0

plants
6.5 _____ 12.0

carp, suckers, catfish,
some insects
6.0 _____ 9.0

bass, crappie
6.5 ____ 8.5

snails, clams, mussels
7.0 _____ 9.0

caddisfly, trout, mayfly, stonefly
(largest variety of animals)
6.5 7.5

Community

Have several students collect and record streamflow measurements.*

Have students measure and mark off a 100-foot distance along a straight section of your stream. If you can't find a 100-foot section, use 25 or 50 feet. Throw a stick (2 or 3 inches long) or a cork in the water above the upstream marker. Record below the number of seconds it takes the object to float downstream between the markers. Divide the 100-foot distance by the total seconds it took the object to float between the stakes.

100 ft ÷ _____ = _____ ft per second
distance   (total seconds   (number of feet
            to float 100 ft)   stick floated
                                  each second)

Find the average width of your section of the stream. Measure the width of the stream at three places within the 100-foot area. Divide the total by three to get the average width of the stream.

First measurement _____ feet

Second measurement _____ feet

Third measurement _____ feet

Total _____ feet ÷ 3 = _____ ft. (avg. width)

Find the average depth of your section of the stream. Meaure the depth of the stream in at least three places across the stream in a straight line. Divide the total by three to get the average depth of the stream.

First measurement _____ feet

Second measurement _____ feet

Third measurement _____ feet

Total _____ feet ÷ 3 = _____ ft. (avg. depth)

*Adapted from the Ohio Department of Natural Resources, Environmental Education Section's stream study material.

Find the number of cubic feet of water moving per second. Multiply the average width, average depth, and the number of feet the object floated per second.

_____ ft × _____ ft × _____ = _____

| Average width | Average depth | Number of feet per second | Cubic feet of water flowing per second |

In order to find out how many people could live from the water in this stream, complete the following calculations. (The average person uses about 200 gallons of water a day in the home. This does not reflect each person's share of water used in industrial, public service, and commercial settings.)

_____ × _____7.48_____ = _____

| Stream flow in cu ft per second | Gallons in 1 cu ft of water | Gallons of water per second |

_____60_____ × _____1440_____ ÷ _____200 Gals_____ = 432

| Seconds in a minute | Minutes in a day | Amount of water one person uses per day |

_____ × 432 = _____

| Gallons per second | | Total number of people who could live from water in this stream |

Part 4: The Biotic Index

The biotic index uses aquatic animals (bottom dwellers) to determine the relative health of a stream. It provides a measure of water quality based on a classification of organisms according to their pollution tolerance. This study, along with the physical characteristics of a stream and the dissolved oxygen content of the water, gives students a very good profile of an important community resource. The following procedure is recommended for this part of the stream investigation.

Collection Equipment

Several pieces of equipment will be needed to collect aquatic organisms. Distribute some or all of these items evenly among teams of 4–5 students: kitchen sieves or strainers, white dishpans of various sizes, collection jars (baby food jars will do), hand lenses, tweezers, and medicine droppers. You may also wish to make a large net, using two sticks that are 2 feet long and a piece of plastic screen about 1 foot by 1½ feet. These dimensions will allow about 6 inches of stick to extend beyond the screen to provide handles. Simply roll one end of the screen over each stick, and tack it in place.

Introducing the Stream

To discourage students from immediately rushing into the stream and disturbing the life in and around it, have them take a few minutes to stop and observe the stream setting, the activity in the air, on the surface of the stream, and in the stream, and the numbers of insects and animals visible before capture. Then establish the boundaries of the stream study and stress the need for the buddy system when working or playing around water. Also stress the great care that needs to be taken when working with tiny animals.

Sampling Procedure

Select sections of the stream that have pools, riffles, and straight stretches. Assign collection teams to each section. Using tweezers, medicine droppers, kitchen strainers, and so on, have teams collect one example of as many organisms as they can find.

If the stream is a swift-flowing, stony brook, have students collect organisms by hand picking them from stones, logs, and any other drifting materials. They must lift larger stones to look for crayfish, which generally lie below the stones waiting for food. The smaller stones will often have smaller insects and small crustacea on them, especially if algae are attached to the stones. Many small tube-like structures are attached to the stones; sometimes they are built from small bits of gravel and plant material. These are the homes of caddisflies and larvae. Have students scoop some mud from the bottom of the stream with the kitchen sieve. Run water through it and, after the mud is washed out, pick out the specimens.

Determining the Biotic Index (BI)

After obtaining a thorough sampling, have the students use tweezers and hand lenses to separate the animals into classes according to the pictures on pages 173–174. Further identification of benthic organisms is provided for your own information on pages 175–177. The grouping of these organisms can be done in the field or back in the classroom.

Class 1 organisms are pollution intolerant.

Class 2 organisms will survive in low levels of pollution.

Class 3 organisms are capable of withstanding adverse conditions within the aquatic environment. They are given a value of zero and do not affect the equation.

When the organisms have been separated into classes, the biotic index may be computed using the following formula:

2 (number of types Class 1 organisms) +
(number of types Class 2 organisms) = BI

For example:

Stream Sample	**Class 1**	**Class 2**	**Class 3**
	3 stoneflies	1 blackfly	1 leech
	1 clam	2 crayfish	2 midges
	2 caddisflies	1 flatworm	1 limpet
	1 mayfly nymph		2 mosquito larvae

2 × 4 (number of types Class 1) +
3 (number of types Class 2) = 11 BI

BENTHIC ORGANISMS

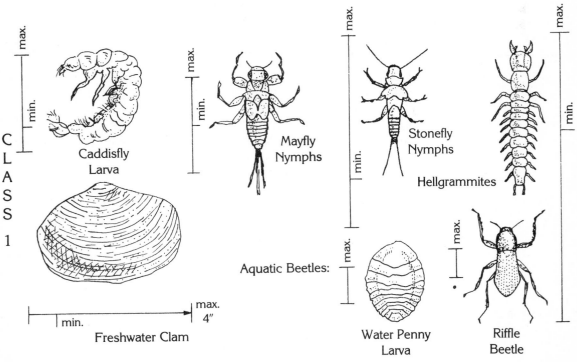

Caddisfly Larva

Mayfly Nymphs

Stonefly Nymphs

Hellgrammites

Freshwater Clam

Aquatic Beetles:

Water Penny Larva

Riffle Beetle

CLASS 1

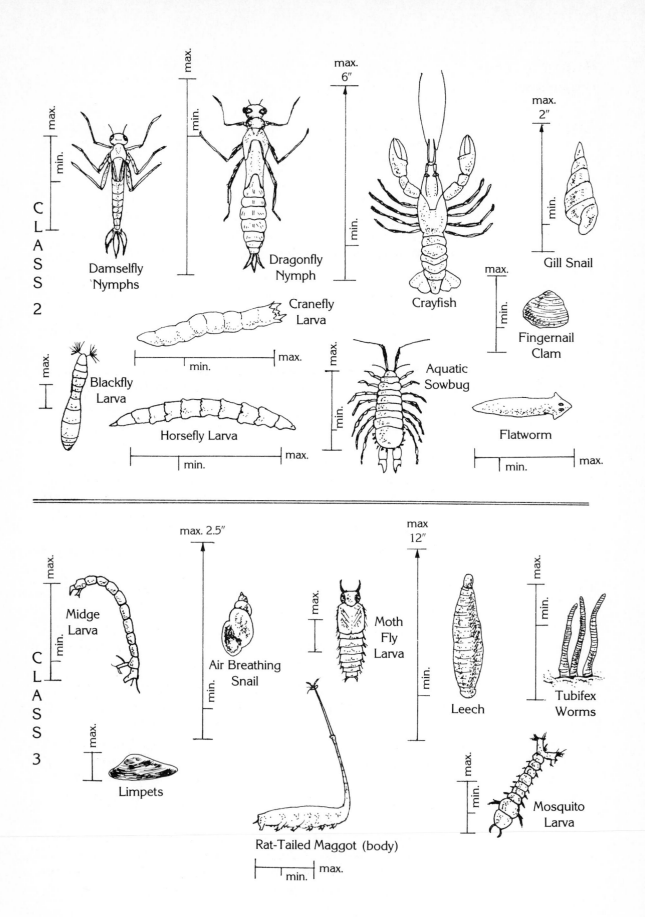

CLASS 2

max.
min.
Damselfly
Nymphs

max.
min.
Dragonfly
Nymph

max. 6"
min.

Crayfish

max. 2"
min.
Gill Snail

Cranefly
Larva
min.   max.

max.
min.
Blackfly
Larva

Horsefly Larva
min.   max.

max.
min.
Aquatic
Sowbug

max.
min.
Fingernail
Clam

Flatworm
min.   max.

CLASS 3

max.
min.
Midge
Larva

max.
min.
Limpets

max. 2.5"
min.
Air Breathing
Snail

max.
Moth
Fly
Larva

max 12"
min.
Leech

max.
min.
Tubifex
Worms

max.
min.
Mosquito
Larva

Rat-Tailed Maggot (body)
min.   max.

Benthic Organisms

Class 1

Caddisfly Larva   Caddis worms or stickworms live in brooks and streams. They live in cases or tubes which they construct from pieces of wood, leaves, and little pebbles. Most larvae are 1/4 inch to an inch in length.

Mayfly Nymph   There are many shapes and sizes of mayfly nymphs, and over 700 species in North America. They have 2 or 3 long slender featherlike tail filaments and one claw on each foot. Most are ½″–1″ in length, but some species are as long as 2″.

Stonefly Nymph   Stonefly nymphs have flattened bodies with 2 tails. They have 2 claws on each foot, while mayflies have only 1 claw. Stonefly nymphs vary in size from ½″ to 2″. These nymphs hatch out in water and live there for a year or more.

Hellgrammite (Larva of dobsonfly)   Full-grown hellgrammites are 2–3 inches long. In May or June when they are about three years old they crawl out on shore or under a stone to pupate. Their large jaws extend fiercely when attacking mayflies and stoneflies. They are used as bait by fishermen.

Freshwater Clam (Mussel)   Mussels are the only other fresh water mollusks besides the snails. They are either rather large, dark-shelled mussels which burrow in muddy bottoms or finger-nail clams lying on the bottoms of brooks or streams (see finger-nail clams in Class 2). All have two shells and a soft hatchet-shaped foot. The largest of the adults is about 4 inches in length.

Aquatic Beetles

Riffle Beetle   These small beetles are about a quarter of an inch long. Their bodies are covered with silken hairs.

Diving Beetle   These make up the major group of water beetles. Their heads form the point of a wedge, with the hind legs bladed like oars. They are ¼″ to 1″ in length.

Water Penny   These flat, copper-colored larvae of the riffle beetle cling to the dark under surfaces of rocks. They live in rapid currents and feed upon the algae film on the stones.

Whirligig Beetle   Whirligig beetles are blue-black or bronze, oval, and flattened. They are easily recognized by their whirling, circling motion on the surface. They are ¼″ to ½″ in length. Front legs project from the sides of the body just behind the head.

Scavenger Beetle   Scavenger beetles resemble diving beetles but with short, club-shaped antennae. They also differ from diving beetles in that they rest in a heads-up position when they are at the surface rather than head down. They are ¼″ to 1″ long.

Class 2

Damselfly Nymph/Dragonfly Nymph Both dragonflies and damselflies usually pass the winter as nymphs in the mud bottoms of streams. Dragonfly nymphs usually require a longer time to mature than damselfly nyphs. They are the dominant insect carnivores of ponds, brooks, and streams.

The damselfly's body is slimmer and more delicate looking than the dragonfly. Three leaf-shaped gills extend from the hind end of the abdomen. It averages ½″–1″ in length.

The dragonfly's body is generally large and chunky in comparison to the damselfly. The dragonfly nymph has no external gills. It averages 1½″–2″ in length.

Crayfish This crustacean looks and behaves like a miniature lobster. It has five pairs of legs with a head and thorax combined or "cephalothorax." It ranges in size from ½″–6″.

Gill Snail Snails are found in shallow waters (1–6 feet deep) where algae and water plants, their main food supply, are abundant. They have a single (univalve) drab-colored shell. Gill snails have a horny plate on the upper surface of the foot near the rear end. The size varies from the Valvatidea Family (prominent keels or ridges on the outer surface, ¼″ shell) to Viviparidea Family (globular or top shaped shell not more than 2″ long).

Blackfly Larva Seen together, blackfly larvae look like swaying greenish-black moss on rocks in waterfalls and rapid streams. A sucker end of each larva attaches to rocks and the mouth is free to take in diatoms. Less than ¼″ in length.

Cranefly Larva Found under rocks, in debris, and in muddy bottoms of streams, the cranefly larva is larger than a midge, brownish to whitish and often quite transparent. There is a breathing disk at the end of the tail. The larva is usually ½″–1½″ in length. The giant cranefly is very large (often more than 2 inches long) and very common.

Horsefly Larva These organisms live in stagnant water, on banks of drainage and irrigation ditches, small streams, and farm ponds. They breathe air through a pair of openings. They are usually ½″ in length, but some species measure 2″. They have a whitish and wormlike shape with roughened ridges around the body.

Aquatic Sowbug Aquatic sowbugs have flattened bodies with head and thorax combined, forming a cephalothorax. They have seven pairs of legs with the first pair modified for grasping. These crustaceans crawl over muddy bottoms eating dead leaves and refuge. Gray, heavy-looking, they measure about ½″ when mature.

Fingernail Clam The two-piece (bivalve) shells of these clams are white or yellowish in color. Their form is similar to the larger clams, but these are usually less than ½″ long; one of the largest measures ¾″.

Flatworm Flatworms are flattened, unsegmented (no rings) worms. Planaria is the common one and looks like a small leech. They have a triangular head and commonly measure about ½″, but some species are up to an inch long.

Class 3

Midge Midges are slender and worm like. Their colors vary, but many have larvae which are blood red and are called bloodworms. Many midges cover themselves with soft dirt tubes. They feed upon algae and decayed vegetation. These larvae vary from ⅛″ to 1″.

Air Breathing Snail The enclosed air chamber of these snails can hold enough air to last a long time under water. Air breathing snails do not have a horny plate (operculum) like the gill snails. They vary in length from ⅕″ (hairy wheel snail) to 2½″ (great pond snail).

Moth Fly Larva These larvae inhabit sludge of ponds, sewage lagoons, and pools of streams. Most forms measure less than ¼″ long.

Leech Leeches are flattened, ringed worms that have a tail and mouth sucker. Leeches feed on the blood of vertebrates and scavenge and prey on other aquatic invertebrates. They vary a great deal in size from ¼″ to over a foot in length.

Aquatic Earthworm These are segmented worms, usually less than 1″ long, but may be up to 4″ in length. The tubifex worms are a common variety. They are slender, reddish worms that dig heads about 1″ in soft bottom mud. Hind parts of bodies extend, forming reddish patches on the mud. These tube-building worms are about 1½″ long and feed on decaying organic matter.

Limpet A limpet is a snail with a lung sac like an air-breathing snail, but it also has a cone-shaped gill extending out beyond the shell. These snails are small, with a shell about ⅕″ long.

Rat-Tailed Maggot This is the prone fly larva which inhabits stagnant waters, pools of streams, marshes, and lagoons. It has a tail-like air tube and the larva measures a little more than ½″ long excluding the tail. It feeds on decaying organic matter.

Mosquito Larva Mosquito larvae are commonly called wrigglers because of their wriggling motion as they swim. These larvae appear hairier than midge or cranefly larvae. The head and thorax are large with a slender abdomen. Air tubes are at the tail end. They feed on minute plant and animal cells and on submerged plants. Larvae are ¼″ to ½″ in length.

Community

References (Benthic Organisms)

Amos, William H. *The Life of the Pond.* New York: McGraw-Hill Book Company, 1967.

Hausman, Leon A. *Beginner's Guide to Fresh-Water Life.* New York: G.P. Putnam's Sons, 1950.

Needham, James G. and Paul R. Needham. *A Guide to the Study of Fresh-Water Biology.* Oakland, California: Holden-Day, Inc., 1962.

Ross, Herbert H. *A Textbook of Entomology.* New York: John Wiley and Sons, Inc., 1967.

Usinger, Robert L. *The Life of Rivers and Streams.* New York: McGraw-Hill Book Company, 1967.

The higher the biotic index number, the healthier the stream. A figure of 10–15 usually indicates a healthy stream. Effluents and other stresses on the aquatic environment decrease diversity: the number of species declines, but the population of those species that tolerate such stresses increases.

Part 5: Dissolved Oxygen Content

Dissolved oxygen is commonly used as a guide to determine general water quality. It measures the amount of oxygen in the water and, as a rule, the higher this level, the better the quality of the water.

Many of the wastes that pollute ponds, streams, and lakes are organic; that is, they originate from plant or animal sources that were alive at one time. When these decompose or decay in a body of water, the process of decay uses up the dissolved oxygen. Untreated or partially treated human wastes, food processing wastes, farm run-off, algae, and so on use up oxygen when they decay. Therefore, a low dissolved oxygen reading implies the existence of a nearby source of organic pollution.

If the dissolved oxygen content falls to a very low level or, even worse, to zero, fish cannot survive because they cannot breathe. In addition, the process of decay changes and further decay occurs. This type of decay produces many of the unpleasant odors (such as the rotten egg smell) that accompany polluted water.

A high dissolved oxygen content indicates either the absence of organic pollutants or sufficient re-aeration (as in a bubbling brook). Concentrations of 7–8 milligrams of oxygen per liter of water (7–8 parts per million) generally indicate water of sufficient purity for recreational use.

Equipment and Materials

We suggest using one of the following kits to determine dissolved oxygen content.

Dissolved Oxygen Test Set
(Range: 04–20.0 ppm.)
Nova Scientific Corp.
111 Tucker St.
P.O. Box 500
Burlington, North Carolina
27215

Water Test Kit
Educational Modules, Inc.
Rochester, New York 14608

Death of a River
Science Kit, Inc.
777 East Park Drive
Tonawanda, New York
14150

Sampling Procedure

Carefully go over the instructions provided with the test kit. Caution students about the use of chemical reagents. Remind them to wash their hands immediately after using the chemicals. Tell them not to get the chemicals on their skin or in their eyes or mouth. If they do, they should immediately wash the area with cool water.

Have students work in small groups of three or four, collecting and testing water samples at the same locations listed for pH and temperature readings.

Record these readings in parts per million (ppm) with other data on the Stream Investigation Data Sheet.

Stream Investigation Data Sheet

Location of Water Sample	Time Taken	Temperature (°F or °C)		pH	Dissolved Oxygen (ppm)
		Water	Air		

Total number of people who could live from water in this stream _____

Streamflow Results

average width of stream _____

average depth of stream _____

water flow _____ cu ft/sec

Questions and Discussion

After returning to the classroom, have each group report their findings to the entire class. Compare their results. The following questions may help to guide further discussion.

1. What might account for any differences in results from each group?
2. What can you say about the quality of the water in this stream?
3. What else do you need to know to decide whether or not to drink the water?
4. Under what conditions might you expect to get different test results than you did today?
5. How can you summarize your investigations today?
6. What processes and methods did you use to find things out?
7. What could you do to improve the stream environment?
8. How could you involve the community in improving the stream's quality?

Options and Extensions

Other water quality tests can be added to this investigation, such as determining the amount of hardness or the quantity of chlorides and phosphates present in the water. Water pollution projects are ideal extensions of this study.

Food chains can be identified and related to energy cycles. Influences that have affected this stream environment can be studied.

Knowing the Night

Purpose To develop an appreciation and familiarity with the out-of-doors at night, to gain a new level of awareness in this setting.

Description A group of students is led through a variety of natural settings—woods, meadow, ravine—at night. Students focus on a series of experiences that heighten the senses and build a new awareness of night.

Materials Small knapsack, flashlight, candle, matches, sprigs of mint, small wintergreen or peppermint candies.

Process During the day, lead the students through a carefully selected area, telling them they will be following the same trail at night. Periodically stop and examine natural features—the sound of a stream, the smell of a pine grove, a clearing in the woods, and the edge of a meadow. At one point along the trail, have each student select an individual tree. Encourage the students to focus on their tree's texture and size, arrangement of branches and leaves, and the environment at the base. Explain to them that they will have to locate their tree again during the night hike.

Shortly before going on the night hike, allow students to share their thoughts and experiences of the night. Discuss the importance of remaining quiet and maintaining silence throughout the hike. Emphasize safety. Flashlights are not needed (though the leader should carry one as a precaution). Check to see that students have proper clothing and footwear.

After the students have had an opportunity to discuss their feelings about the night, assemble outside away from as many lights as possible. This will enable the group to develop their night vision. Mood becomes important at this point. The leader should soften her or his voice and encourage a respect for silence. Take a final count of students and have them line up in single file or in pairs.

Move slowly along the trail and stop at various points to interpret what is there. What was obvious during the day becomes strange and different at night. Encourage the students to focus on patterns and shapes, the dark and light shadows, changes in temperature, the contrast in smells, and the symphony of night sounds. For example: What shapes do the leaves and branches make against the night sky? What temperature differences do you notice? Does the forest appear closer to the trail now? What new sounds are you aware of? Have the students cup their hands behind their ears and bend them forward slightly. This will accent sounds in an interesting way.

At the selected point along the trail, have students locate the trees examined earlier in the day. Encourage them to focus again on their trees' characteristics, contrasting the day and night's awarenesses. End this phase of the hike by having the students sit down at the base of the trees and experience the forest night in silence. Reassemble the group and continue to stop at various points along the trail to continue experiencing and interpreting the night.

Near the end of the hike, group together in a circle for a few final activities. Light a candle and pass it around. As each student holds the candle, have them reflect on the night hike. Pass a sprig of mint around the circle and have the students comment on their awareness—smell, touch, and taste. Calling in an owl is an exciting experience, and inviting along a naturalist who "gives a hoot" will long be remembered by the group. A sparkling activity the students enjoy is watching each other crunch down on wintergreen or peppermint candies in the dark. It is necessary to keep the mouth partially open to witness the fireworks. (The combination of sugar and mint when crushed causes a phosphorescent-like flash.)

Options and Extensions

The night hike can end around a campfire with a story or poem, or have the students write poems or paragraphs about their night hike experiences.

Notes on the use of Discovering the Community activities:

Bibliography

Allison, Linda. *The Reasons for Seasons.* Boston: Little, Brown and Company, 1979. Stories to read, ideas to think about, and things to make and do all contribute to an understanding of the seasons and their effect on the earth.

Arnocky, Jim. *Outdoors on Foot (A Book of Nature Crafts).* New York: Coward, McCann, and Geogheaga Inc., 1978. The delights to be found on a nature walk are highlighted.

Bonsall, George. *The How and Why Wonder Book of Weather.* New York: Wonder Books, 1971. Good background on weather, clouds, winter, and snow is presented.

Busch, Phyllis. *Once There Was a Tree.* Cleveland, Ohio: World Publishing Company, 1968. The story of how a living tree becomes a log and how it interacts with animals and other plants in the environment.

Chernoff, Goldie. *Pebbles and Pods.* New York: Walker and Company, 1973. Clever illustrations and easy-to-follow instructions make this a cut above other craft books. Readers are encouraged to make things from materials found outdoors.

Cooper, Elizabeth K. *Science in Your Own Back Yard.* New York: Harcourt, Brace, & World, 1958. Well-organized, easy activities are featured, including how to build a backyard laboratory.

Cornell, Joseph B. *Sharing Nature with Children.* Nevada City, Calif.: Ananda Publishing, 1979. Teacher resource.

Darst, P.W., and G.P. Armstrong. *Outdoor Adventure Activities for School and Recreation Programs.* Minneapolis, Minn.: Burgess Publishers Co., 1980. Program planning, teaching strategies, environmental concerns, and information on activities for outdoor programs are included. Teacher resource.

Davis, Hurbert (ed.). *A January Fog Will Freeze a Hog and Other Weather Folklore.* New York: Crown Publishers, 1977. A delightful book centering on American weather folklore and its history; well documented and beautifully illustrated. All ages.

Frankel, L., and G. Frankel. *101 Best Nature Games and Projects.* New York: Sterling Publishing Company, 1959. Observation and nature-study games for partners or small groups are presented. Teacher resource.

Graham, Ada. *Foxtails, Ferns, and Fish Scales (A Handbook of Art and Nature Projects)*. New York: Four Winds Press, 1976. Projects are presented for each environmental section. Teacher resource.

Hammerman, D.R., and W.M. Hammerman. *Teaching in the Outdoors*. Minneapolis: Burgess Publishing Company, 1973. Introduction to outdoor education offers effective techniques and procedures and suggestions for organizing, implementing, and evaluating outdoor programs. Teacher resource.

Harty, William. *Science for Camp and Counselor*. New York: Association Press, 1964. Good weather section, including designs for weather instruments. Teacher resource.

Hillcourt, William. *The New Book of Nature Activities and Hobbies*. New York: Putnam, 1970. Hundreds of nature and conservation projects focusing on various topics are described; project checklists and many references are included. Teacher resource.

Hopf, Alice. *Bugs, Big and Little*. New York: Simon & Schuster, 1980. Explains what insects are, examines interesting facts about them, and discusses collecting and displaying them.

Howe, Leland, and Mary Martha Howe. *Personalizing Education*. New York: Hart Publishing Company, 1975. Strategies on how to clarify values and suggestions for developing classroom interaction are presented. Teacher resource.

Hug, J.W., and P.J. Wilson. *Curriculum Enrichment Outdoors*. New York: Harper & Row, 1969. More than 350 activities for the different subjects are listed according to grade level. Teacher resource.

Joseph, J.M. *Point to the Stars*. New York: McGraw-Hill Book Company, 1972. Clear instructions on how to find the constellations and interesting background information about each of them are presented.

Koff, Richard M. *How Does It Work?* Garden City, New York: Doubleday & Company, 1961. Explanations of weather, humidity, rain, thunder and lightning, thermometers, and weather reports are given.

McMillan, Bruce. *Apples. How They Grow*. Boston: Houghton Mifflin Company, 1979. A description and illustration of how apples grow from bud to fruit. All ages.

Musselman, Virginia W. *Learning about Nature Through Crafts*. Harrisburg, Penn.: Stackpole Books, 1969. Good information on insects and a variety of activities are presented.

Nickelsburg, Janet. *Nature Activities for Early Childhood*. Menlo Park, Calif.: Addison-Wesley Publishing Company, Inc., 1976. An excellent source for activities and information on nature presented clearly; aimed at younger children. Teacher resource.

Pettit, Ted. *A Guide to Nature Projects*. New York: W.W. Norton & Company, 1966. Weather and insect information and experiments are presented for upper elementary and junior high level students.

Pringle, Laurence. *Discovering the Outdoors*. New York: Doubleday & Company, 1969. Great photos and investigation ideas make this an exceptional nature guide for field studies.

Ronan, Colin. *The Stars*. New York: McGraw-Hill Book Company, 1966. This is a picture book about the stars.

Rush, Jennifer. *The Beginning Knowledge Book of Backyard Trees*. New York: Macmillan Publishing Company, Inc., 1964. Nice illustrations will encourage young readers to find out more about their neighborhood trees.

Russell, Helen Ross. *Ten-Minute Field Trips*. Chicago: J.R. Ferguson Publishing Company, 1973. This is a teachers' guide to using school grounds for environmental studies; includes good weather activities. Teacher resource.

Scandone, Thomas F. *Emphasis: Natural History*. Palo Alto, Calif.: National Press, 1967. Manual for students with little or no biology background includes good examples of integrating classroom, museum, and field experiences.

Schneider, Herman. *Everyday Weather and How it Works*. New York: McGraw-Hill Book Company, 1961. How to read a weather map and how to make and use weather equipment for different experiments are explained.

————. *Science Fun with a Flashlight*. New York: McGraw-Hill Book Company, 1975. Experiments with a flashlight, demonstrating concepts about light, shadow, color, the sun, the moon, and much more are suggested.

Schramm, Wilbur. *Classroom Out-of-Doors*. Kalamazoo, Michigan: Sequoia Press, 1979. The organization, coordination, and activities of the San Diego City-County school camping program for sixth graders are described. Teacher resource.

Shuster, C.M., and F.L. Bedford. *Field Work in Mathematics*. New York: American Book Company, 1935. Practical applications and activities on measurement, the use of instruments, mapping, and so on are presented.

Shuttlesworth, D.E. *Exploring Nature with Your Child*. New York: Harry N. Abrams, 1977. This focuses on teaching children to appreciate nature; good photographs. Teacher resource.

Simon, Seymour. *Animal Fact/Animal Fable*. New York: Crown Publishers, 1979. The validity of common beliefs about animals is explained.

————. *Exploring Fields and Lots (A Handbook of Simple Projects)*. Chicago: Garrard Publishing Company, 1978. Young children explore fields and vacant lots and record their findings about plant and animal life.

Smith, Howard. *Hunting Big Game in the City Parks*. New York: Abington Press, 1969. Habits and habitats of insects, their scientific and native names, their hunting methods, and instructions for making an insect zoo are presented.

Swan, Malcolm D. (ed.). *Tips and Tricks in Outdoor Education*. Danville, Illinois: Interstate Printers and Publishers, 1970. This book includes how to approach outdoor education; materials, ideas, and worksheets for a variety of outdoor activities for different subjects; ideas for planning, conducting, and following up field trips. Teacher resource.

Van Matre, Steve. *Acclimatization*. Martinsville, Indiana: American Camping Association, Bradford Woods, 1972. The classic outdoor education book, this provides a sensory and conceptual approach to ecology and outdoor study. Teacher resource.

Wensberg, K.S. *Experiences with Living Things (Introduction to Ecology for 5–8-year-olds)*. Boston: Beacon Press, 1966. This presents classroom and field activities, annotated bibliography for teachers, bibliography of children's books, and suggested poems and stories to use with each activity. Teacher resource.

Wolff, Barbara. *Evening Grey, Morning Red*. New York: Macmillan Publishing Company, Inc., 1976. Weather predictions are colorfully illustrated and explained in words that primary students can read and understand; a good weather folklore resource book for teachers.

Zappler, G., and L. Zappler. *Science in Summer and Fall*. New York: Doubleday, 1974. Descriptive chapters cover a broad range of topics on discovering and understanding natural objects in back yards and vacant lots.